FROM PEN TO PENSION

A true story of the ups and downs
of a career in banking during a period of
unprecedented change in the financial
affairs of post-war England.

By

Roger Howard F.C.I.B. (retired)

Grosvenor House
Publishing Limited

This book is published by
Grosvenor House Publishing Ltd
Link House
140 The Broadway, Tolworth, Surrey, KT6 7HT.
www.grosvenorhousepublishing.co.uk

A CIP record for this book
is available from the British Library

ISBN 978-1-83975-389-3

Dedication

This book is written for the benefit of my five grandsons, Jack, George, Finlay, Harry and Thomas, but is dedicated to my dear wife Maggie, who supported me throughout my career but who is now residing in a lovely care home as a result of developing semantic dementia some twelve years ago. I am lucky enough to have two wonderful daughters, Sarah and Alison, and their husbands, Adam and Matt, and they all contribute to making my declining years so perfect.

Foreword

At a time when the country is locked in a fight against a worldwide pandemic that threatens the future of many, it is perhaps appropriate to record the past that has, since the Second World War, demonstrated the ability of man and woman to recover and thrive following setbacks of historic proportions.

This book is a brief record of events and developments in the banking industry as seen during a period of forty post-war years when the world economy recovered with the help of developments in engineering and technology, all of which occurred at a rate so fast that it was almost impossible to keep up.

It is not intended as a detailed record of those developments, rather it is a memoir of a journey through a banking career which started at the very bottom and which led to management of one of the largest branches of Barclays Bank in the south of England.

As children we were never quite aware of what our father got up to after he dropped us off at school. Now we know!

Sarah Shave and Alison Roberts.

Preface

Ever since retiring in 1993 from a forty-year career in banking, I have toyed with the idea of recording the events, incidents and anecdotes which contributed to such an enjoyable and satisfying career experience.

As the country moved from post-war austerity to an explosion in technology, the bank had to respond to ever-changing circumstances. A near-death experience, spending thirty-three days in Frimley Park hospital, followed by enforced isolation during the coronavirus pandemic, prompted me to embark on this true story of the ups and downs during a career which started at the age of just sixteen and that culminated in early retirement some forty years later.

The story spans forty years, during which growth in the banking habit took off, to such an extent that very few people manage without a bank account today, unlike 1952, when anyone with a bank account was regarded as either in business or very wealthy.

Having been retired twenty-seven years, I believe that I can express an honest opinion on my former colleagues without damaging them, plus, I have avoided naming anyone in the hope that no offence will be taken. I have attempted to present a candid account of life working for Barclays, but any errors must be blamed on the passage of time and are entirely innocent.

Introduction

I must start by admitting that my education left me little prepared for a career in banking as I achieved only three G.C.E.'s: Mathematics, English and Art. I had to sit an English and Mathematics entrance exam to gain employment with Barclays Bank, and thus began an exciting, if slightly unconventional, career that lasted long enough to secure a full pension representing two-thirds of my final salary...something that not many working today will enjoy.

Throughout my career I took seriously the adage that "my word is my bond", a phrase that has little significance today. I stuck stubbornly to what I believed to be right and failed to toe the line when those in authority were, in my view, wrong. This uncompromising attitude led to many standoffs and gave rise to many ups and downs in my career along the way, and eventually led to my early retirement.

As I did not keep a diary, the specific dates and times of events may not be exact but the record is as near as I can remember and I have tried to state facts without exaggeration. This book may never see the light of day but I hope it will provide enjoyable reading for my family, to whom it is dedicated.

Chapter One

Bethnal Green branch

Year 1952
Prime Minister, Winston Churchill
Inflation Rate: 4.33%
All Share Index: 46.59
Base Rate: 2.5%

On Friday 19th September 1952, a letter arrived from Barclays Bank. I opened it with trepidation as I had already been turned down by Midland Bank, and believed that my lack of educational qualifications were insufficient for the career I was seeking. I had taken an entrance exam, whilst I was confident of how I had done in the Mathematics test, the English test, details of which I can't remember, was a much weaker subject of mine.

Much to my surprise and satisfaction, I was invited to join the bank staff at the Bethnal Green branch on the following Monday. As I did not have a suit I made a hurried visit to Fifty Shilling Tailors, where suitable attire was purchased. The suit was slightly short in both the arms and legs but my mother made the necessary alterations, so as to avoid any embarrassment, as I embarked on a career that was to last forty years.

I was informed that my salary would be £170 per annum, plus £50 per annum London allowance. Payday was then, and always has been, on the 23rd of the month so, a day after starting, I received my first salary. By my calculation that was around £4. 16 shillings and a penny. In those days there was a two old penny stamp duty on all cheques. To avoid the cost of the stamp duty, staff were allowed to withdraw cash of £1.19.11, i.e. one old penny under two pounds, on a debit slip. Two pounds and over would give rise to the two old penny stamp duty. That duty was abolished on the 1st February 1971, shortly before decimalisation.

At the age of just sixteen, I had never been inside a bank and knew very little of what would be expected of me. The careers master at my Grammar School had a good line of jobs in shipping offices, but I decided I did not want to do what my school friends were doing and, with the encouragement of a family friend, decided that banking might be the answer.

I should mention that my father died when I was aged eleven and there was really no thought of trying to get into a university. As a family we struggled financially and as far as I can remember, my mother received a widow's pension of just ten shillings (50p) a week. Fortunately, my father's employers, Ilford Ltd. (the film company), offered my mother a job which meant we had enough income to survive.

With the start date being of such short notice, I had no chance of visiting Bethnal Green beforehand and arrived in a strange area ringing the front doorbell with considerable nervousness. I received a friendly welcome and soon discovered that I suffered a serious handicap in the fact that I was left-handed. Biros had not been invented yet and I was required to use a pen and ink to write in customers passbooks. Anyone who is left-handed will understand how difficult it is to write with your left hand as there is a tendency to smudge your writing as your hand passes over what you have written. I also discovered that the only mechanical equipment, an adding machine, was designed for right-handed people, as the lever was on the right-hand side.

My duties included copying records from ledgers into customers passbooks and onto handwritten statements, as passbooks were gradually being withdrawn. I was also responsible for operating the telephone switchboard and listing cheques in the clearing received in a daily delivery from head office. The clearing cheques represented cheques drawn on the branch that had been paid into other branches and banks. They were then sorted into alphabetical order and listed again before they were posted in very large and heavy loose-leaf ledgers.

The bank's doors were opened at 10 am, with all activity over the counter being recorded in the Cashiers account books and then placed in a wire basket. The credit slips and details of the makeup, i.e. cheques and cash, were then handwritten on to large sheets known as waste sheets, so that all of the transactions were on record. All cheques paid into the bank were then sorted into the various banks and listed for submission to head office and placed in the head office letter bag at the end of the day. The incoming cheques, known as remittances, had to be listed and balanced with the total recorded on the waste sheets, which was my prime responsibility. Essentially everything had to balance, cash in and out as well as cheques in and out, before we could head home. Clearly, whenever there was a discrepancy, departure in the evening was delayed. If it was not possible to leave early there was a tendency to hang on until after 6 pm to earn two and sixpence (half a crown or 12.5p in today's coinage) in tea money.

The manager usually arrived sometime after the staff. He had a very loud voice, something which I was to learn quickly when I tried to operate the telephone system, which I found completely beyond my ability. Despite being shown how to operate the system, each time I tried to put a caller on hold whilst I announced his name to the manager I somehow managed to cut the caller off, after which there would be an explosion from within the manager's office when he found that no one was on the line. I got to the stage where I was frightened to operate the system which was not very user friendly.

Within a few days I was informed that I had been sent to the Bethnal Green branch by mistake and was asked to report to the Upton Park branch, which was also in an area which I was totally unfamiliar with.

I briefly returned to the Bethnal Green branch on relief, but the manager and I had an understanding that I would not touch the telephone system. Beneath that gruff exterior was a man with a heart, and I held him in high regard.

Chapter Two

Upton Park branch

Year 1952.
Prime Minister, Winston Churchill
Inflation Rate: 4.33%
All Share Index: 46.59
Base Rate: 2.5%

I had such a brief start at the Bethnal Green branch and was rather unsettled by a move to another branch so quickly. As with Bethnal Green, I had no knowledge of the new area in which I was to operate. Had I known what I was in for I might have taken fright. The branch was adjacent to a bus terminus which had a direct impact on the branches daily business.

Most bus journeys then cost between one and two old pence, hence, there was a huge amount of copper coins that ended up at the bus terminus, and thereafter at the bank. Currency in the 1950s comprised of copper and silver coins, with pennies being one of the largest and heaviest coins. There were 240 pence to the pound, with copper coins being large and heavy, unlike coins today. Each day, vast amounts of copper coins were deposited into the bank and they all had to be stored in the strong room, beneath the banking hall, ready for the weekly collection by a security van. Part of my responsibility was to transport the incoming coins down some rickety wooden stairs into the strong room. The only aid provided was a trolley and a small manual lift, which had no brake and had to be wound up and moved at a snail's pace as I struggled to turn the large metal handle. Woe betide anyone who let go of the handle, as the lift would return rapidly to the basement. Due to the weight of the coins in the lift, any attempt to grab the fast-spinning handle could severely damage either your arm or fingers. Once the lift reached the top it was possible to lock it into position.

I quickly concluded that, although I might use the lift once or twice, my strength could not stand much more, so I used to carry the cash bags up and down the stairs, finding myself cream crackered by the end of the day. The weekly collection of incoming coins required transporting it to the top of the stairs, in readiness for the arrival of the security van, where it would be placed on the trolley and wheeled out to the van. On one occasion I stacked the bags so badly that a number of them fell down the stairs. To demonstrate the weight involved, not only did they fall down the stairs but they fell through the stairs, breaking the wooden steps, which had to be repaired. I stopped stacking them at the top of the stairs.

My abiding memory of my, thankfully, brief time at the Upton Park branch was the considerable manual element of my duties, and even though there was a Bank

Messenger there to help, he never seemed to be around when the heavy work commenced.

The First Cashier was an elderly, rotund man who liked to have his fun. As 5th November approached, he decided to let off a jumping cracker in the banking hall. After having just cleaned the area the Messenger was rather put out by having to clean up the mess. Two days later as the First Cashier was balancing his till the Messenger surprised the cashier by letting off a banger behind him. I have never seen anyone come so close to a heart attack. Thereafter there was a clear rift between the two men that lasted for the remainder of my short stay at the branch.

On one occasion, in mid-winter, I was, in the absence of the Messenger, requested to light the boiler. Despite many efforts with wood and some sort of anthracite, my attempts were unsuccessful and I was blamed for the staff having to work in their overcoats for the day. The Messenger informed me upon his return that the only way to light the boiler was with a bit of coal, which he kept in a bag and of which I was completely unaware.

In addition to the heavy manual work, I was expected to undertake similar duties to those I had undertaken at the Bethnal Green branch, which were relatively easy, although not always completed without errors. This gave rise to efforts to identify why things failed to balance by calling back the cheques against the listings. I quickly learned that poor handwriting led to such things as fives looking like eights, sevens looking like twos or ones, and fours looking like sixes.

My subsequent transfer to the Shoreditch branch came as a relief and provided probably the most amusing period of my early banking career.

Chapter Three

Shoreditch branch

Year 1953
Prime Minister, Winston Churchill
Inflation Rate: .38%
All Share Index: 40.17
Base Rate: 4.00%

Until I worked at the bank, I had always regarded bank premises as something akin to the church, where everything took place in hushed and ritual ways, where little fun was had by anyone. This was not the case at the Shoreditch branch. The main banking hall was long and narrow, with the cashiers to the left of you as you entered the bank. Behind the cashiers sat the Ledger Clerks, all young men who had recently completed their national service. They were responsible for recording cheques in the morning clearing in the large loose-leaf ledgers and for posting items presented over the counter during opening hours: 10 am until 3 pm. The cashiers were all men in the final years of their banking career and were led by the First Cashier, a man who enjoyed a drink or three during his lunchtime which, all too often, was spent in the taproom of the local Courage brewery directly opposite the branch. Many an afternoon was spent, post bank closure, in encouraging the First

Cashier to sing bawdy songs and quote humorous rhymes, of which he seemed to have an endless supply. On occasions he produced a rubber model of a man's genitals, I think it was called a "dill doll", which he banged on his desk before throwing it around the office, generally in my direction, as the males attempted to hide it from the few girls who worked in the branch. I can still hear the banging now, which was a sign to standby ready for the missile. Occasionally he had a bonfire of the many broken paper cash bags, with the encouragement of the Ledger Clerks, who challenged him to get the flames above the level of the desks so that they could see them. The entertainment did not occur every day but often enough to lighten our working environment.

This all too brief activity soon subsided as the ritual of checking the referral cheques took place. At 3.30 pm the Manager, Assistant Manager and Chief Clerk, arrived in the middle of the ledger desk to decide which cheques would be returned due to lack of funds. As the cheques were posted in the ledgers, posters checked the balance to ensure that it was within the lending limit. If not, the cheques were tucked into the top of the ledger so that the Manager could go straight to those accounts with cheques sticking out of the ledger. It seems that many of the customers were aware of this ritual and, on occasions, the doorbell would ring and a desperate customer would produce some funds of some sort to ensure that his cheques were honoured. Cheques that were returned had to be despatched in the post to the appropriate banks with a note on them indicating the reason why they were returned.

My responsibilities included providing the Manager with a cup of tea mid-morning, which was obtained from a street trader outside the branch who offered a range of drinks, sandwiches and snacks. By the time the tea reached the Manager's room, most of it was in the saucer and had to be poured back into the cup. Staff members were allowed to visit the local Jo Lyons for a morning tea break, and on one occasion I was given a telegram to send via the Post Office during my break. Much to my horror, I found the telegram in my pocket a week later and decided the best thing was to send it. Fortunately, there were no repercussions; I expect the delay was blamed on the Post Office.

I was also responsible for listing the cheques received in the daily head office bag, before sorting them into alphabetical order and listing them again before they were passed onto the Ledger Clerks. There was usually a huge amount of these and there was help available to ensure that the clearing (incoming items from the bag) balanced before the cheques were posted to the various accounts. The bank was beginning to mechanise its operations with bank statements and daily, over the counter, transactions being recorded by German-built Mercedes machines that were operated by girls who seemed particularly adept at posting with speed and accuracy.

Once the clearing had been dealt with, over the counter business began to give rise to significant volumes of cheques being drawn on the various banks. These (remittances) had to be sorted into bank order and listed in readiness for despatch in the head office letter bag at the end of each day. These remittances were summarised, with the total having to match with the daily record of business from the waste sheets before they could be packaged together and put with other items in a canvass bag. The bag was then sealed with a wax seal and sent via the postal service.

I blotted my copybook very early on when the books were balanced too late for the postal service. I was instructed to deliver the bag to the clearing department in the city, where I had never been before, and I had great difficulty in finding the office, which was closed by the time I reached it. Much to the horror of the Chief Clerk, I arrived at the office the following morning with the bag. I do not know how the matter was sorted out but I was never asked to undertake a delivery again.

As I was awaiting the chance to start my National Service, those who had completed their service ragged me about the experience I could look forward to. I was frequently informed that I would have a very tough time, with a sergeant yelling at me on the parade ground as I was knocked into shape. Little did I know that those words would help me get off to a good start, purely by chance, once I had been recruited into the Royal Air Force.

My experience at the Shoreditch branch was not without incident as I, on one occasion, managed to set light to the Head Office letter bag. Unfortunately, the incident was spotted by the Chief Clerk who gave me a telling off. The contents of the bag were, fortunately, undamaged, but the canvas bag was beyond repair.

Everything for dispatch to Head Office was placed in a basket on a window sill, immediately behind me. I have already mentioned that the bag was sealed with wax and as a non-smoker I did not possess any matches. Alongside the basket containing the bag was a small gas burner, which I kept alight, although turned down very low, so that I could melt the wax. Someone must have brushed past the gas burner, which was on a swivel, and it came to rest against the full bag awaiting dispatch. Needless to say, the gas burner was never left on again.

Probably the worst incident to occur, and for which I got blamed, arose when a small team of builders visited the branch to carry out a check on the building, prior to a substantial refurbishment programme. A member of the team mentioned to me that he would be cutting a small hole in the ceiling behind me from upstairs, and I said that was OK. I continued to machine list the remittances and did not notice that the Chief Clerk was on the internal telephone, which was directly beneath the intended incision. The Chief Clerk completed his call and stepped away just as a huge chunk of masonry landed exactly where he had been standing. There was an immediate enquiry and it was pointed out that I had been informed of the investigatory work. I don't think I was ever forgiven. On reflection I really do not know what was expected of me, was I meant to stop work and watch for the "small hole" to appear? In those days there was no such thing as "health and safety".

Shortly after the incident I was called for an interview at Head Office, I was expecting to be informed that I was not considered suitable for a banking career. Instead, the interview was to tell me that I was now a permanent member of staff having completed, and passed, my probationary period.

I left the Shoreditch branch with many happy memories as my National Service approached. It had been fun and laughter accompanied by some serious practical experience of how the banking system operated.

Chapter Four

National Service

Year 1955

I commenced my National Service training in the R.A.F. at West Kirby, on the Wirral peninsular, and until today didn't realise exactly where it was! After kitting out, we had our first lecture on the parade ground, before marching off to our accommodation. I can remember a corporal shouting at us with words I will not repeat, but it was exactly as my former colleagues had described, and I allowed myself a brief grin which was immediately noticed by the corporal. He made me march to the front and asked me my name and why I was smiling. I cannot recall my reply. We were then marched to our billet and, to my surprise, the person in the first bed was made billet orderly and as the corporal knew my name I was made deputy. Both positions had a few perks as we were responsible for maintaining the cleanliness and appearance of the accommodation for weekly inspection. We were not required to undertake the work but acted as overseers and wore our first badge of authority, in my case a white armband. That smile had worked to my benefit. Fairly early on an officer inspected the room and complained of the poor standard of presentation. I felt that it fell to me to point out that my fellow recruits had worked very hard and I did not feel it was as bad as he described. The officer turned a bright shade of puce and tore me off a strip. Subsequently, the corporal in charge of our billet told me I was very lucky not to be put on a charge.

The highlight of the week was pay parade. When our names were called we had to march to a table, piled with coins, salute and shout out our service number before receiving the princely sum of eight shillings, four florins (40 pence today). On one occasion a serviceman approached the table, did a very smart salute and slid into the table which was loaded with florins, sending them in all directions, much to the delight of all those waiting. The ritual was held up for some considerable time before order was restored, much to the embarrassment of those in charge.

During our basic training we spent a weekend in the Welsh hills, in the depths of winter, under canvas. There was snow on the ground and each billet was split into two, led by the billet orderly and his deputy. The team leaders were called together for instruction whilst the teams erected the tented accommodation. The senior officer later observed that a tent was going up on its own some considerable distance from the main encampment. My group had decided they wanted some privacy but, of course, they had to relocate alongside the rest, which meant that the tent had to be re-erected after dark. Not a good start. The following day each group was set the task of map reading and locating defined villages, as well as undertaking suitable research into those villages. We were under strict instructions not to enter public houses. My group, under my control, reached its destination with little difficulty, and the public house seemed the ideal source of information. We thought we could find all of the information we needed with the help of the locals and a pint or two. We were later joined by an army officer who was friendly and was not part of our R.A.F. Unit. Little did we know that he must have been spying on us, because when we returned to base, we found ourselves in trouble for disobeying orders. Our punishment was to dig the latrines, but I am sure we were not the only ones to use our initiative in such circumstances.

As far as I can recall basic training took six weeks and ended with a passing out parade before we were all posted to units according to our choice of specialism within the services. I had decided that I would avoid anything clerical and opted for training as a radar operator. My posting was to R.A.F. Bawdsey, the first fully operational Radar Station in the world, just north of Felixstowe, across the River Deben. I believe that R.A.F. Bawdsey played a key part in the "Battle of Britain", which was a major turning point in the Second World War.

The base consisted of small bungalows accommodating groups of four to rooms with shared washroom facilities and toilets. The accommodation was some distance from the underground radar station and we were required to march to and from there as we undertook our training and subsequent duties. As the work entailed a lot of concentration, gazing at a radar screen, we worked alternate mornings and afternoons, with the possibility of night work after our morning duties. We were allowed to remain in bed after working nights, but not on any other occasion. Although there was little else for us to do, we very often remained in bed, even when we were not working nights, but this was risky.

From time to time the billets were inspected and anyone found in bed was put on a charge. Fortunately, our accommodation was not the first in line and a warning would be issued that an inspection was underway. In such circumstances there was no time to get dressed and make up the bed. The only way to avoid being caught was to strip the bed and head for the toilets loaded up with our bedding. Many a time a bunch of us stood on the toilet seat, holding our breath and trying not to laugh, with someone, trousers down, sat on the loo. I am not sure whether anyone knew what was going on. It certainly gave us a feeling that we had one up on the inspecting officers.

As we had a lot of time on our hands, we had gambling groups playing pontoon and brag. Part of my service education taught me the bluffing skills needed for such card games and we always welcomed any regular servicemen who had money to burn. If we won, we would enjoy a night out in Felixstowe at the weekend. Otherwise, we would remain on camp if we did not have a weekend pass. Getting to and from Felixstowe entailed travelling across the river Deben in a small open ferry boat with a small outer platform, which it was necessary to step onto before climbing aboard. This was relatively easy when sober but there were many wet accidents on the return journey, much to the amusement of the other passengers.

As the weeks went by, we made our evenings more enjoyable by producing food as we participated in these card games. The food was obtained from the mess, by hiding it on our person, after the evening meal. It developed to a stage where someone would be delegated to stand outside the mess to await a loaf of bread that would be thrown from a window. Unfortunately, fairly early on, the man responsible for collecting the loaf saw an officer approaching and, deciding he might be caught, left the scene. The loaf was duly thrown from the window and was spotted by the officer who attempted to find out who was responsible. No one admitted responsibility, but this ended a very useful supply of toast for our evening comforts.

Certain precautions were needed when taking a bath as, for a brief period, someone had the bright idea of sticking a firework in the overflow pipe from the bath. Successive people got caught as the filthy contents of the overflow pipe were fired into the bath. We all began to hang a flannel over the overflow exit, with the culprit eventually giving up.

The radar operator training went smoothly, with some being better at it than others. An operator was expected to read the movement of an aircraft, shown as blips on the screen, to someone known as a plotter, so that each aircraft position could be shown on a huge map in the central control room.

Somehow, I showed promise as a radar operator as my readings were fast and accurate. Like in many situations, if you are good at your job you are moved on to higher things, and I was invited to become the Chief Controller's assistant. The Chief Controller had a small room, known as a cabin, set high, overlooking the control room floor, opposite a large screen which identified the aircraft activity that was under the station's control.

I was expected to deal with all of the flying activity, by telephone, to the various airfields, and inform those operating the screen, over a loudspeaker, what needed to be displayed. Fortunately, the telephone system was not as complicated as that at the Bethnal Green branch. The Chief Controller had overall control over flying activity while other junior officers spent most of their time doing practice interceptions (PI's): taking one aircraft into an arc and directing the other to intercept at the right time, with the correct height and speed. It was an art that many found difficult and I had a "fly on the wall" position to hear all that was going on and learn exactly what the boss thought of their efforts. There were times when other information was displayed on the wall screen, it was usually cricket scores or other important news items.

As part of his responsibility, the Chief Controller (C.C.) had the May Day channel constantly open, with there being some exciting moments from time to time. One in particular comes to mind, when a rather concerned pilot reported that he was lost and was running low on fuel. In a very calm manner, the C.C. asked him to fly in small circles so that we could see him on our screen. We had the whole of England on the screen and waited for a blip to make a circular movement. Nothing showed up, and as the pilot became increasingly frantic, I thought to myself, it's easy to be calm when you are safely on the ground. Eventually, the pilot bailed out safely with his plane crashing into the sea; it turned out that he was flying over France, and must have passed over the Channel in cloud. I never learned the outcome of any enquiry that must have taken place following the loss of a valuable aircraft.

During my time at Bawdsey, we sent up an escort to accompany a Tupolev Tu-104 from Russia, which was to bring Bulganin and Khrushchev to the U.K. in 1956. It was one of the few occasions that we identified the aircraft on the chart as a hostile, which showed up as a black H on a yellow background.

In addition to being at the centre of things, there were perks to my position. I was required to be in position before the others arrived and as a result of this was given an excused marching chit and was driven back and forth from our accommodation to the base. I was also responsible for getting the weekend passes signed by the Chief Controller, and there was the occasional comment concerning the frequency my name cropped up. I had a good relationship with my boss and this showed when my discharge report was sent to the bank. The Staff Manager informed me that he had never seen such a good report, and I did point out that we worked together for a long time.

On one occasion, in mid-winter, with snow on the ground, we decided to prepare a large snowball which I threw at the female group, as we drove past, as they marched to the radar station. Unfortunately, the missile missed the marchers and hit the corporal in charge, reducing her to tears. I was punished and had to clear snow from the entrance to the base rather than perform my normal duties. I do not remember whether my boss passed any comment, but there were no other repercussions.

I look back on my two years of National Service with very happy memories, where I learned to mix with the rich and poor, and discovered many ways of getting one over on those in charge. As far as I was concerned National Service was something that should have been continued. It was character building and knocked people into shape, with an eclectic mix of young men who learned much from mixing with people they might not usually come across. There was a mutual respect amongst national servicemen and I think that many of the youth problems today would be avoided if something similar was still in place.

Chapter Five

East Ham branch

Year 1957
Prime Minister, Sir Anthony Eden
Inflation Rate: 2.99%
All Share Index: 62.37
Base Rate: 5.5%

During my two years of National Service, the mechanisation of branch banking had progressed to the extent that the heavy ledgers had disappeared, with ledger sheets being kept in trays and all entries being machine printed. I returned to find hardly any other developments and was back listing the morning clearing cheques, like I was before, and the incoming remittances for dispatch in the Head Office letter bag.

Outside of London there was something known as local clearing, which involved all cheques received over the counter being drawn on local banks. They were treated separately and were listed by the bank and branch for exchange the next day at a brief meeting of representatives from all the local banks. Bankers payments were issued in settlement for cheques drawn on the other banks and the cheques were then exchanged and returned to the branches on which they were drawn.

On one sunny morning I set off to attend the usual meeting with the cheques and necessary bankers' payments in a leather wallet. All was right with the world as I returned to my branch from the exchange and opened the leather wallet only to discover it was empty. Panic took over as I realised that I had deposited the entire contents along the high street and, in my ignorance, I imagined people picking them up and paying them in, or at the very least taking them home. I rushed to the bank entrance and into the arms of a man who, thankfully, had been following me, picking them up as I dropped them. Never in my life have I been so relieved at such a swift turn of events. Fortunately, nothing was missing and to this day, I do not know whether I thanked the man sufficiently for saving my bacon.

During my time at East Ham, my career progressed to Cashier and then First Cashier. It was good to come into direct contact with customers and I enjoyed the challenge of balancing my till at the end of the day. All cashiers make mistakes and tills did not always balance. I made my fair share of errors, and from time to time minor discrepancies occurred which were never found. Anything above ten pounds was cause for concern but two notes stuck together or miscounted, could give rise to shortages or even work out in the bank's favour.

The East Ham branch had one customer who was a constant cause of angst to the cashiers as he always arrived near closing time and was loaded up with wet notes and a very nasty smell of fish. None of the cashiers wanted to serve him as it took a considerable amount of time and delayed the balancing of the individuals till. As you will surmise he was a fishmonger, and at a time when weighing notes was becoming the norm, it was quite impossible to do anything other than count the notes which were wet, stuck together, covered in fish scales and only fit for destruction. As closing time approached, all of the cashiers would become aware of his presence due to the smell, and in order to avoid him we all tried to hide beneath the counter, with the unlucky cashier rising to find him standing at their position.

There was a small incident that was to work to my benefit one Christmas when one or two salary increases were awarded. I was made aware that one of the cashiers had received a rise of £10, I felt aggrieved that I had missed out. I mentioned it to the Manager who convinced me that it was not worth making a fuss about. I accepted his advice in the hope that I would not be overlooked the following year. Subsequently, the Manager was promoted to a job in the Head Office staff department. The fact that I raised the matter was to work to my advantage at a later date.

During my two years at the East Ham branch, I started attending evening classes so I could take the banking exams, and despite my poor educational qualifications I passed all exams over a four-year period, failing in only one, finance of foreign trade, once.

The banks' premises were ageing and there was a dire need to replace the piping which passed through the strong room where all the cash was held. Workmen started to remove the old piping and discovered that the walls of the strong room were weak, as a result, a large hole developed. The poor Chief Clerk got into serious trouble when he reported the matter to Head Office the following morning. Head Office felt that something should have been done on the evening of the discovery. Huge, free-standing safes were delivered to the bank that same evening. A passenger on the top deck of a passing bus, saw the safes being rolled into position and phoned the police, thinking they were being removed. The police surrounded the bank and a small report of the event appeared in one of the National newspapers. However, this was not the end of the matter as work on the strongroom ran into the evening. About a week later a customer, about to deposit his days' takings in the night safe, heard drilling and reported it to the police. Once again, the branch was surrounded and the workmen either could not hear the doorbell or were reluctant to respond so it took some considerable time to sort things out. The poor Chief Clerk took the blame for the lax communication and had a tough time for some weeks.

On another occasion one of the major pub chains was collecting a substantial sum to distribute to its Christmas club members. We observed a suspicious car opposite the branch, with four men inside, so phoned the police, only to discover that it was their plain-clothes squad keeping a watchful eye on proceedings, as the pub chain had informed them of the substantial cash movement.

My departure from the East Ham branch came suddenly when I was asked to immediately go to the Stock Exchange branch in the City, where there was a crisis. I was not being transferred but was being sent on relief with the expectation that I would return. I never did!

Chapter Six

Stock Exchange branch

Year 1959
Prime Minister, Harold Macmillan
Inflation Rate: 1.40%
All Share Index: 74.57
Base Rate: 4.00%

I believe I arrived at the Stock Exchange branch mid-afternoon and joined a team, gathered together from various branches, who were tasked with dealing with a long list of differences dating back some months. The branch itself was in chaos, because in October Harold Macmillan had won the third election for the Tories and the stock market took off. The system in operation allowed customers to instruct branches to buy and sell shares with the instruction then passed on to the Stock Exchange branch who dealt directly with the market. Suddenly the branch was inundated with instructions and anyone who was near a phone had to record a branch request and pass it through to the dealers. Those requests gave rise to additional work as settlement took place, and quickly the branch became overwhelmed, not just with instructions, but with the volume of work associated with a huge increase in activity.

The team, of which I was a member, worked hard to bring into balance work where there was insufficient time available to deal with differences on the day they occurred. An account which was titled "overs and shorts" recorded all of the differences. Gradually, we worked through the past accounting records and ate into the huge list of errors. I cannot recall whether we balanced everything, but we certainly got things back into control.

As the team started to dwindle, I was asked if I would stay on as a cashier. I formed the conclusion that the cashier team was not a good career move, with them eventually offering me the job of Assistant Supervisor, which was a much better opportunity, and which, in my view, helped to galvanise my career in a timely fashion. The Supervisor was responsible for the accounting side of the banks business. At the Stock Exchange branch it was a very responsible position as we were dealing with huge sums of money, and were involved with major stockbrokers who demanded a very high standard of service.

Within a very short amount of time, I became Supervisor and made many changes to what I considered to be Dickensian practices. My short time as Assistant Supervisor gave me the chance to look carefully at the management decisions that were ill thought out and did little to ensure the smooth running of the accounting department. In addition, the brokers were also under pressure and often demanded bank statements, expecting the cheques to be in line with the statement. Frequently, statements were not properly checked and the banks answer to a complaint was to have them checked by yet another person before they were dispatched. As mistakes had been repeated on many occasions the list of names to check became so huge that there were about six people checking. With all members of staff under pressure, many assumed that someone else had done the checking, with this assumption in fact resulting in a total failure of the system.

As Supervisor, I immediately made both the person issuing the statement and one named checker fully responsible so that there could be no short cuts. Mistakes were greatly reduced, but there was something else causing distress and low morale. Copies of all correspondence were circulated to the management daily, and any letter of apology to a stockbroker gave rise to an inquest with the person or persons responsible, subject to carpetting by the Manager. I took the decision to ensure that no copies of letters of apology were circulated, and thus avoided any repercussions. As far as I am aware, the management never realised my action, but it made my life a lot easier and the work of the staff a lot less fraught. Perhaps it also gave the Manager the impression that the office was operating more efficiently than was the case.

I have already mentioned the Dickensian practices that existed and the standard letters, which must have stood for many years, were extremely out of date. We used expressions such as "we beg to enclose" and "we are your humble servant" and many others that were, in my view, an embarrassment. Standard letters were rewritten, and slowly the branch was brought into the twentieth century.

The first Christmas under my control was a nightmare. On Christmas Eve I had to go into the local pubs and drag staff members back to work after their lunch break. The management ran a draw for a number of bottles which were gifts from the brokers and, unknown to me, the junior won a bottle of port, which he consumed with one of the junior girls during his lunch break. After the management had departed for their holiday, I was left to sort out a days' work carried out by members of staff who were a little worse for wear. This meant more than the usual number of mistakes. Furthermore, I learnt that both junior members of staff had been sick in the bank basement and the female was presented to me in a terrible state. I took the blame for the mess in the basement and was blasted by the messengers who had to clear it up. By that time I had given up the will to live and I asked those who knew the young lady to put her on a train which would stop at her station. My Christmas was completely spoiled by what occurred and I felt let down by the management who were unaware of the result of their actions.

On my return to work after Christmas, I made it clear that under no circumstances could the events of Christmas Eve be repeated. Furthermore, I expected the management to remain within the branch until it was clear that the work of the day was in balance.

I cannot pretend that I had an easy time initially when I was promoted to Supervisor. There was an unwritten agreement that no one went home until all the work was balanced. Two troublemakers attempted to ignore that agreement and together persuaded another member of staff to join them departing for home without my knowledge or permission. In my view, they were trying to undermine my position and I marched them into the Manager's office the following morning. Later, I was informed that all three had resigned. After a discussion with the Manager, I advised that two could go but I wanted to retain the one who had been led astray. The Manager agreed that he would give the one a chance to change her mind, which she did, while the others had the indignity of having to ask if they might withdraw their resignation requests. From that day on I had no difficulty in controlling a very busy office.

As I continued my job as Supervisor, there were events that are worthy of record. We were a Town Clearing branch and cheques, I believe that were worth over £5,000, were cleared the same day, with smaller cheques going through the normal system. It had always been surprising to me that our banking hall became packed with brokers just as 3 pm approached, and it took us much effort to record the high-value cheques and have them ready for clearance by 3.15 pm. It was not until I discovered, by chance, that Barclays was the only bank prepared to keep its doors open beyond 3 pm that I realised we were suffering as a result of our generosity. As a consequence, we were left to the end when it came to brokers rounds. On learning of our soft approach to locking the doors, I let it be known that our doors would no longer remain open beyond 3 pm. Problem solved, the pressure eased, and a practice that had existed for years suddenly halted.

To demonstrate the volume of activity through the branch, there was an occasion when the Manager received a call from the Chairman's office to inform him that the bank had fallen below the 8% cash level we were expected to retain with the Bank of England. We were informed that research suggested that it was down to our branch. After all the waste baskets were checked that contained incoming items over the counter, we discovered something at the bottom of one of the baskets. It contained cheques to the value of more than £5 million. These were quickly taken around the city for clearance, and the banks reputation was restored.

A few months into my employment at the branch, the bank undertook a complete review of all of the salaries and nearly everyone received a modest increase in pay. The Manager had a list, and called members of staff into his room to inform them of the increases. Long before it was my turn, I was advised, by someone who obviously could read upside down, that I was the only one on the list to receive three figures. I later found out that my salary had increased by £100, which was well above all the others on the list, and a not inconsiderable boost to my salary in those days. I have no doubt that my old Manager at the East Ham branch, who was now working at the staff department, had come up trumps!

During my spell in the City, I learned a little about the activities of the stock exchange, and purchased some shares in Butlins. Little did I know that one day I would meet Sir Billy Butlin, who was a very loyal customer of Barclays. I attended the annual general meeting as part of my education and felt very important as I marched through a line of redcoats to listen to the great man report on his company's success.

It was during my time at the Stock Exchange branch that I completed my Institute of Bankers exams, which meant I was an Associate Member of the Institute of Bankers and could put the letters A.I.B. after my name. I was now safely set on a long-term career in banking. The Institute of Bankers received its Royal Charter in 1975, and the letters changed to A.C.I.B.

The Stock Exchange branch was located in Angel Court, behind the Bank of England, surrounded by high buildings, which prevented much natural light entering the building.

My departure from the Stock Exchange branch was brought about by exceptional circumstances. I arrived for work one Monday morning to find that there had been a complete power failure, leaving the branch in semi-darkness with none of the accounting equipment working. Not only were we, as a branch, completely knocked out, but, coincidentally, the bank's inspection team descended on us. I asked the inspectors if they could delay their visit but was informed that the inspection must continue. With the help of hurricane lamps, torches and anything which provided some sort of light, we commenced the business of the day. All the work had to be transferred to other city branches, with staff and messengers deployed around the City to ensure that the days' work was recorded on appropriate accounting equipment. Suitcases were provided to carry everything to the assisting branches and it was, in my view, a challenge that the staff enjoyed, and in which they all played a significant part. Much to my surprise and satisfaction everything balanced the first time, a rare event even in normal circumstances. Whilst I cannot claim any special plaudits for the outcome, it was clear that I benefitted from this outcome, so much so, that I was invited to join the inspection team very shortly afterwards. I was then sent to the Mile End branch to learn about securities work; a part of my training that was sadly lacking. So, I started what I like to consider as phase two of my banking career.

Barclays Bank Limited.

STAFF DEPARTMENT, HEAD OFFICE.

JLH/RGJ.

54, Lombard Street.
(ENTRANCE GEORGE YARD)
London, 18th September, 1952.
E.C.3.

R.L. Howard, Esq.,
9, Aragon Drive,
Barkingside,
Ilford, Essex.

Dear Sir,

With reference to your application for a post on our Staff, we now have pleasure in informing you that you have been appointed to a Clerkship on the Permanent Staff of the Bank, the first six months of your service to be regarded as a period of probation.

Your commencing salary will be at the rate of £170 per annum and you will receive the appropriate London Allowance of £50 per annum whilst you are attached to the office to which you are now appointed. As already discussed with you, you will also receive such Cash Payment as may be declared by the Board; at present this is paid on a ~~quarterly~~ basis.
half yearly

This engagement is subject to one month's notice of termination on either side and to the regulations and conditions of service obtaining from time to time. You will be required to sign a Staff Agreement and to subscribe to the ~~Guarantee and~~ Widows' Funds in accordance with the rules. In this latter respect, the Secretary of the Funds will be communicating with you direct.

Will you please report to the Manager, Barclays Bank Limited, 349, Bethnal Green Road, E.2. at 9 a.m. on Monday the 22nd September taking this letter with you as a means of introduction.

Yours faithfully,

ASSISTANT STAFF MANAGER.
P. T. O.

Letter of appointment

37

National Service, the Author complete with white armband

ROYAL AIR FORCE

R.A.F. FORM 1394.
(Revised December, 1981.)
(For issue only to National
Service Airmen and Airwomen
not on regular engagements).

BRIEF STATEMENT OF SERVICE AND CERTIFICATE ON DISCHARGE

1. Surname _HOWARD_   Official No. _2745672_
   Christian Names _ROGER LESLIE_   Rank on Discharge _S.A.C._
2. Period of whole-time service. From _22-1-55_ To _3-1-57_
3. Trade in civil life _BANK CLERK_   4. R.A.F. trade on entry _Aft Kas 55_
5. Details of any R.A.F. trade training
6. R.A.F. trade on discharge and brief description of duties. (vide A.M. Pamphlet 51.)

7. Assessments of Conduct, Proficiency and Personal Qualities during service :—

	Exemplary	Very Good	Good	Fairly Good	Poor
(a) Conduct	X				

	Exceptional	Very Good	Good	Fairly Good	Poor
(b) Ability as tradesman/aircrew* *Delete as inapplicable		X			
(c) Ability as supervisor in his trade *(Applicable to N.C.O.s only)*		✓			
(d) Personal Qualities :—					
(i) Leadership			X		
(ii) Co-operation	X				
(iii) Bearing (to be assessed " Very Smart," " Smart," or " Untidy ") _Smart_					

8. Medals, Clasps, Decorations, Mentions in Despatches, etc. _Nil_
9. Reason for Discharge _COMPLETION OF WHOLE TIME NATIONAL SERVICE_
10. REMARKS. (This section to be used only to amplify Assessments, trade qualifications, etc., where necessary.)

11. DESCRIPTION ON DISCHARGE
    Height _5_ ft. _11_ ins.   Colour of Hair _Brown_
    Complexion _FRESH_   Marks or Scars _Various_
    Colour of Eyes _Blue_
12. National Service airmen are liable to undergo part-time service—See notice overleaf.

UNIT DATE STAMP
17 JAN 1957

Signed _____ Rank _____
Commanding _ROYAL AIR FORCE BAWDSEY_

Signature of Airman/Airwoman _____

(*3724—1203) Wt. 38973—BJ 1055 3,200 Pads 5/54 T.S. 839

National Service Discharge Papers

39

Presentation to Alan Ball, Manager of Portsmouth FC

Speakers at Institute of Bankers biennial dinner

Chapter Seven

Mile End branch

Year 1961
Prime Minister, Harold Macmillan.
Inflation Rate: 1.72%
All Share Index: 106.37
Base Rate: 5.00%

The Mile End branch is situated on Whitechapel Road, directly opposite the Blind Beggar public house, which earned notoriety when Ronnie Cray murdered George Cornell some five years after my brief training period, which was aimed at preparing me for a transfer to the bank's inspection department.

I found the branch to be an ideal training ground with a wide range of customers, from street traders to professional workers, both rich and poor. The Securities Clerk dealt with the assets accumulated by customers in the form of shares, property and other forms of savings. Many of those assets would be pledged to the bank, in support of overdrafts and loans, which gave rise to the preparation of documents safeguarding the bank's position. Life was made more complicated by the introduction of stamp duty, linked to the amount borrowed, and even though I managed to master the system it has now become a very grey area in my memory and has, I believe, since been abolished.

During my very short term at Mile End, I joined the Poplar Round Table, which was a new branch of that organisation in the East End of London. I had my first public speaking experience when I was asked to propose a toast to the guests at the inaugural dinner to celebrate the formation of a new table. My life experiences up to this point and my education left me totally unprepared for such an event, and I learned quickly not to fix my eyes on anyone, casting my eyes over the audience from side to side. Apart from knowing that I needed to stand up, speak up and shut up, I approached the event with considerable trepidation. Much to my embarrassment, I ignored the microphone, not realising that my voice faded as I directed my gaze from side to side. The situation was rescued by the master of ceremonies who was directly behind me, and ensuring that the microphone remained in front of my mouth. That experience caused me to approach speeches later in my life with a degree of nervousness, which often put me off the food that was in front of me on such occasions. As a result, I spoke at both my daughter's weddings, before the meal, so that my enjoyment of the event was not spoiled. My membership of the Round Table was something that I never regretted; it was extremely advantageous to my career, as I moved from branch to branch, as it gave me an immediate group of like-minded friends, many of whom were involved in the community. Not only did it incorporate a part of the activities involved in raising money for local charities, it provided a chance for me to get involved, at a very early stage, in a new community.

There were few incidents worthy of note, but on one occasion the Manager told us that a customer approached him with a suitcase full of cash. He reported that a similar case had been stolen from his property but he didn't want to report it to the police as he had been sorting it away to avoid tax. Serve him right! The problem was resolved by the purchase of a large deed box and the funds were placed with other boxes, contents unknown, in the bank's strong room. I believe the loss was in the region of £7,000, a not inconsiderable sum in those days. He would have done better to pay his taxes!

I do recall that the biro had just been invented as a wealthy customer who visited the branch weekly, to sign documents in connection with his investment, kept reminding me that his biro was still working. That invention was a boon to left-handers like me and probably never got the plaudits it deserved.

The Mile End branch was a very brief interlude and a learning experience which helped me to deal efficiently with customers' needs in a way that was advantageous both to the customer and the bank.

Chapter Eight

Inspection

Year 1962
Prime Minister, Harold Macmillan
Inflation Rate: .67%
All Share Index: 118.47
Base Rate: 6%

My move into Bank Inspection, initially in London, was again a learning process, but there was an element of excitement as we lurked outside the selected branch in readiness to pounce at 9 am on the unsuspecting staff. The inspection started by checking all of the cash in all of the tills and in the strong room. It was often very clear, at the initial stage, whether the branch would be found in good order, as signs of problems were often apparent from day one.

Inspections were very thorough and although some of the work was mundane and repetitive, the examination of the lending record often made for interesting results. All inspectors used green ink biros so that they could make their mark on the branch's financial records.

Banks around this time were in the early stages of computerisation. In fact, Barclays was the first bank to introduce an electronic computer in 1959, and developed a purpose-built computer centre in 1961. I did have an opportunity to visit the computer centre, a large building, which had huge electronic machines in specially cooled premises, which, within a few years, was operating from only half of the ground floor. There was a problem for all banks, as computerisation was developing at such a rapid rate that it was difficult to decide when to take the plunge and opt for a system that would soon become outdated. There is, however, little doubt that computerisation and the introduction of the internet many years later revolutionised the banking system and enabled it to grow to a stage where there are very few citizens without a bank account today.

My spell in London was short-lived as I was asked to join the Southampton inspection team where I came across the now District Inspector, who undertook the inspection of the Stock Exchange branch and recommended me for a move onto a team. I do not know whether I joined him by accident or design but, even though it was an unexpected move, I found a new life outside London, and one which was a delightful change from commuting into the smoke.

I secured digs in Southampton very close to the Dell, which at that time was the football ground for the City team.

My first branch inspection in the South was the Bournemouth main branch and, compared with travelling into London, a morning drive through the New Forest was quite beyond my best expectations.

Working on inspections gave me a thorough knowledge of the whole Southampton region, which spread from Bognor to the East and Poole in the West, taking in Salisbury, Winchester, Petersfield and Midhurst to the North and included the Isle of Wight and the Channel Islands. Possibly the best region in the country, in my opinion. The area was controlled by the Southampton Local Head Office, where the inspection department was based.

Essentially the inspection teams were the banks internal auditors, I probably learnt more about the inner workings of the bank during my three and a half years as an inspector than I learned at any other time during my career. After an initial period of learning on the job, I was made an Assistant Inspector and was allowed to head up the team on smaller branch inspections. I can clearly remember my first assignment, we arrived on time at 9 am, before the strong room was even opened. I witnessed the young lady insert the key in one lock, it did not turn so she withdrew it and inserted it in the other lock which turned. I asked her into which lock she normally inserted the key and it became clear that the strong room keys had been compromised as she clearly had had possession of both sets of keys at some stage. I was very proud of myself but on reflection I should have been a little more sympathetic to her situation. It was immediately necessary to change the locks.

The inspection team generally travelled in the District Inspector's car, but it gradually became apparent that the District Inspectors driving was not something that any of us enjoyed. There was pressure from all to seek the relative safety of the back seat and eventually I mentioned the quality of driving to the Senior Local Director. He managed, in the most tactful way, to convince the District Inspector that it was sensible to travel separately, and to the relief of many we travelled in comparative safety thereafter. Little did we realise at that time that the District Inspector was suffering from early-stage Parkinson's disease.

Inspection of the Jersey and Guernsey branches necessitated staying away in good hotel accommodation, which was regarded as a working holiday. For branches on the Isle of Wight, we would travel daily on the hovercraft which necessitated finishing early to get the last hovercraft of the day back to Portsmouth. I had one of the early weekly season tickets, I think it was number 5.

My initial attachment to the Southampton inspection team was for a year, which was subsequently extended for the whole period on the inspection team. I liked the area so much I approached the Senior Local Director to see if he could find me a job in the Southampton region. Much to my delight I was offered a job as Chief Clerk at the Salisbury branch as my tour on inspection came to an end. At a subsequent interview, in London to confirm the posting, I was informed that with demand for staff in London being so high, no one ever got permanently posted out to the provinces. Clearly, the Senior Local Director had pulled some strings, something for which I was eternally grateful.

As I left my inspection role, I felt that I had finished the learning phase of my banking career and, although you never stop learning, I was ready for a task where I had the freedom to do things my way.

Chapter Nine

Salisbury Branch

Year 1965
Prime Minister, Harold Wilson
Inflation Rate: .97%
All Share Index: 108.84
Base Rate: 7%

What luck, here I was starting my journey in the Southampton region in the wonderful city of Salisbury. After my first day in the office, I realised that my job would be a doddle as I was replacing a man who had organised everything so that as Chief Clerk he had very little to do. If I was lucky there might be a letter to deal with, but the branch ran like clockwork, and on a good day everyone would be ready to go home by five.

I believe that I was a reasonable boss, but I did come across a young lady who was extremely rude to me in front of the staff. I immediately told her to come with me to a private room, and, leaving the door ajar, reprimanded her in no uncertain terms, informing her that any repetition of that sort of talk would mean she would be out of the bank before her feet touched the ground. I would not have been allowed to take such action but I had got the point across to the staff that even though I might be easy going I would not put up with rudeness of any sort. I think I always found the need to demonstrate a no-nonsense approach when taking on a new management role.

I had found accommodation just outside of Salisbury in a small garage complex which had been previously occupied by a vet. The unit had been refurbished to provide a small bedsit together with an entrance through the garage. The big plus, as far as I was concerned, was that the daughter of the house was a cordon bleu cook. The deal included the provision of an evening meal that I would find keeping warm in my oven on my return from work. I did learn from my landlady, a widow, that she had suffered a tragedy many years ago. She showed me an old copy of the front page of the daily newspaper which showed pictures of her home burning down during which, I learned, her husband suffered a heart attack and died, as he sought to rescue family heirlooms from the burning building. I also noticed the price on the newspaper was 1 1/2 old pennies. Just about 1p in today's money.

My stay at Salisbury was very brief as a Local Director arrived unannounced to see the Manager. The Assistant Manager was out and the Manager was engaged with a customer. As a result, I talked to the Local Director and happened to mention that I was rather underemployed as the branch ticked over very well with little input from me. Some days later the Manager informed me that he did not know what I had said to the Local Director but I was required at Local Head Office that same day for an interview.

Little did I realise that I had been shortlisted for a special job and, as a result of my chat with the Local Director, my name moved to the top of the list. I was required to set up a training school which was to operate out of the Fareham branch, to train staff to manage small branches. The bank had been growing at such a rate, opening more and more branches, but was short of suitably trained personnel to run them. I was given a free hand to develop a training course, fit out a classroom and run it for, I think, a three-month period, with each course lasting, again from memory, two weeks. Lunches were to be taken daily at a good restaurant and there would be some sort of test to ensure that the attendees benefitted from the experience. I immediately set about preparing the course which included a daily head office letter bag both morning and evening, trying to make it like a normal day at any small office. Once all the preparation was done, I was called to present all the details to the Local Directors only to find that what they really wanted to know was whether I would become Assistant Manager of the Winchester branch once my work was completed. I was delighted with the promotion and enjoyed the task of teaching branch management, which I had yet to experience myself, to my colleagues. I also benefitted from the meals provided by an upmarket restaurant, which took place in a private room for course lunches at the bank's expense.

As my time at the Salisbury branch was so short there were really few incidents of note. However, one evening I was in the toilet prior to heading home when there was a panicky knock on the door and a shout from a female member of staff. I emerged to find the Bank Messenger lying in a pool of blood twitching. An ambulance was called and one of the cashiers had had the sense to remove the man's false teeth. It seemed that the Messenger had collapsed and had torn his ear on a nearby desk. I had the unenviable task of driving to his home to break the news to his wife. The news came as no major shock as I learned that he suffered from epilepsy, an illness that he should have declared when he applied for his job.

I was also called out in the middle of the night when the bank's alarm system activated. I found the branch surrounded by police and as I had a key to the door I was invited to go in first. Fortunately, it was a false alarm, but I felt briefly exposed as the first person to enter the premises.

With both a Manager and Assistant Manager on hand to deal with customers, my customer contact was very limited. However, on one occasion I interviewed a customer who wanted to raise some money to develop a new fire extinguisher which he sought to demonstrate to me. He produced a small dish of paraffin, which he lit. Unfortunately, he held the extinguisher too close to the paraffin and the pressure sent the lit paraffin everywhere. After extinguishing the flames dotted about the room without the use of the extinguisher, the customer was sent on his way.

During my National Service I rose to the modest rank of Senior Aircraftsman, now here I was in charge of an office which had retired officers of Wing Commander, two Squadron Leaders and an Army Colonel. As part of their contract, the retired servicemen were not allowed to use their rank. All operated as cashiers and were generally up to the task. It was, in my view, very sensible to use them in a city such as Salisbury, where they could communicate well with the Salisbury clientele. As an aside, all admitted that they had never worked so hard in their lives!

Luck was on my side as the role of Chief Clerk is probably the most difficult on any career path and I had got through it in very quick order. Now, here I was posted to another cathedral city and I took the opportunity to invest in the property market, purchasing a newly constructed two-bedroom flat for £4,000 in Chandlers Ford.

Chapter Ten

Winchester branch

Year 1967
Prime Minister, Harold Wilson
Inflation rate: 3.46%
All Share Index: 111.20
Base Rate: 7%

My move to Winchester at the age of thirty-one, into my first managerial job, was heaven sent. Once again, I was working in an important city and had my own car parking space! Life was sweet and I was working with a Manager who taught me much in the way he handled staff. He was very much a people person who made every attempt to keep the girls happy, even to the extent of patting their bottoms, a practice that would be frowned upon today, but which worked well in the 1960s.

The Manager's daily routine included a morning session in his room, known as prayers, when we reviewed anything of interest from the previous day. The session included coffee and a review of the *Financial Times* by the principal of securities. These sessions occasionally took too long and left me struggling to catch up with my duties. They were, however, useful and became a practice that I adopted subsequently to maintain good contact with my management team. It was at this stage that I took on a lending role which, when it comes down to it, is probably the most important element of banking. Thankfully I did not stay long enough for my lending mistakes to catch up with me as I seemed to be "on a roll" as far as progress with my career was concerned.

In less than a year I was again called to the Local Head Office to be offered the job of Assistant District Manager Advances. My main task was to deal with all advance applications received from the growing number of branches that were within my delegated lending discretions, both secured and unsecured. I cannot recall what my discretions were but the secured element would have been twice the unsecured level, and both would present me with a challenge for which I did not feel fully prepared.

During my spell in Winchester, I joined a badminton club. One evening, whilst driving to my flat after badminton, there was a slight mist and I observed a car very close to my rear end. In an attempt to get away I drove rather fast and it was not until I drove into my garage entrance that I observed that I was followed by what turned out to be a police car. I was informed that I had exceeded the speed limit in Winchester, Hursley and again in Chandlers Ford. After getting over the shock I asked why the police car had not stopped me. I was asked what I did for a living and their attitude changed when I told them I was Assistant Manager at Barclays. I was then informed that if I took my driving license to Winchester Police Station I would hear no more about it. I related these details to the Manager's secretary the following morning only to be informed the following day that her father was Clerk to the Court in Winchester. Her father had expressed concern that the three misdemeanours could give rise to three separate court cases and I might lose my license. He also stated that if he had a pound for every time it had been reported to the Court that the police had said the accused would hear no more about it, he would be a very rich man. Anyway, the Clerk to the Court took the matter to the Chief Constable and I received an assurance that no action would be taken. For a short time I had to consider how I would manage without a car.

There was another problem that pervaded my entire time at Winchester. The telephone switchboard was operated by a young lady with limited eyesight. She started to receive threatening calls against the Manager and was frequently in hysterics. We took the matter seriously and, with police help, installed recording equipment. Despite being shown how to operate the equipment the telephonist never managed to record the threats which she related to the Manager. Matters were made worse when the Manager received a call at his home, and it was not until some time had elapsed that we realised that the telephonist had made the whole thing up to gain attention. By this time I had moved on to my new role in Local Head Office and I never knew who had made the call to the Manager's home.

I felt that my task at Winchester had barely begun and I had not really had sufficient experience of lending.

Now I was on the move to a position where I would be the man to make decisions on many proposals with a lending limit far higher than that I had enjoyed in Winchester. Only time would tell whether I was up to the job.

Chapter Eleven

Southampton Local Head Office

Year 1968
Prime Minister, Harold Wilson
Inflation Rate: 3.65%
All Share Index: 127.90
Base Rate: 8%

I was familiar with the Southampton Local Head Office set up as the inspection department had its base office on the premises. I had also visited, from time to time, for interviews and had been based there previously as I prepared the courses that I ran at Fareham. But now I had my own office within the establishment. My post was a new one, because until that date the existing Assistant District Manager dealt mainly with staff matters, whilst advances were shared between him, the District Manager and the Local Directors.

As more and more branches across the region began to appear, the volume of business increased rapidly, and I took over responsibility for a large proportion of branch lending at the lower range. Applications were submitted on forms 21, which provided information boxes containing the history of accounts together with details of directors, partners, security and other relevant information. A submission contained a summary of the requirement together with the branch managements comments on the borrowing proposal. All new applications were examined by the advances team before they appeared on my desk with an appropriate recommendation. There was, in addition, a large volume of general correspondence covering changes to existing borrowings, temporary excesses, bad debts and all matters pertaining to the bank's lending's.

In addition to my role in dealing with advances, I was at the beck and call of all the Local Directors and was given any rotten job that came into the office that no senior person wished to deal with.

On one occasion we were asked to provide a speaker to give a talk on cash flow management to a national organisation in the Midlands. How it came into Southampton Local Head Office I will never know but it landed on my desk. Fortuitously, *The Financial Times* had produced a very useful article on cash flow, linking it into a domestic water system. They had produced a mock-up of a house together with the plumbing, so I used this, with other slides, to brighten up my presentation. It was not until I arrived at the hotel that I came to realise just how high powered the event was. I was informed that the Finance Director of Dunlop Rubber was there and other public company executives and that the other speakers were university professors. Fortunately, I was to speak first and felt that using *The Financial Times* article duly doctored to make it look like my own, worked pretty well. Having never gone to university, I did not appreciate just how boring a lecture could be. The university lecturers used no visual aids and I came to the conclusion, with all due modesty, that I came out on top.

During my time at Local Head Office or LHO as it came to be known, the banks introduced the Credit Transfer System and once again I was landed with explaining to Peter White, the now well-known blind broadcaster, how it would operate as we spoke for the benefit of his tape recording machine. I had never before spoken into a tape machine but it became normal practise in the office, as secretaries were gradually withdrawn in favour of machines.

The area, or district, was run by the District Manager, with a board of Local Directors headed by a Senior Local Director as a higher tier of management which made major decisions. There was a definite hierarchy and the Directors were very aware of their position. As I got to know them I came to realise that although they were well educated, they were, to some extent, ego-driven, and man-management was not their strongest quality. From time to time, when bad decisions were fed down the line, I became the go-to man who would attempt to change things that were not acceptable to the general office who did the donkey work. On many occasions I would take a trip up the corridor to seek reason, sometimes successfully, sometimes not, but I found it a challenge that I rather enjoyed.

Fairly early on, I was working late and emerged from my office to find all the staff going through the entire filing system. On enquiring what was going on, I was informed that an important file had gone missing and the powers that be, having themselves departed, had decreed that no one could go home until it was found. The staff believed it was locked in a drawer in one of the Director's offices. I took the decision to send everyone home and lo and behold the file was found where the staff suspected. It was silly decisions such as that that undermined the respect that we were expected to have for our seniors.

I must confess that I found my job very high pressured and as a non-smoker, I was given to exploding from time to time. On one occasion, the reason defeats me, I announced that I was walking out and not coming back. I wandered around Southampton for some time before heading home. I believe that the District Manager and Directors had realised they had pushed me too far and I was sent on a few days jolly to Guernsey on the pretext of reviewing the lending book of the former Martins branch. It was not my first visit to the island, as I had visited there whilst on inspection, but it provided a very enjoyable break.

That was not the only occasion I flew off the handle. The bank made a decision to replace all the dictating machines with up to date cassette operated equipment. The old machines, which operated on large open spools, were to be scrapped but to save money the District Manager decreed that LHO would use the old ones until they broke down.

Every half-year I had to prepare a summary of bad debts throughout the district, for submission to Head

Office, and this required a précis of all the reports from all of the branches on the major accounts at risk. I had spent one whole morning dictating into a machine, when suddenly the two reels started spinning and deposited a tangle of tape all over the floor, there was no hope of recovering the recording. In timely fashion, the District Manager, who had been to a working lunch, put his head around the door. He did not know what hit him but from then on all the old machines were removed. I had to start my work again but at least we had achieved a sensible removal of defunct equipment.

It was during my four years at LHO that we moved premises to a new office block in Southampton. Plans for the new offices were drawn up with neither me nor the Assistant District Manager staff being consulted. Much to our horror, we discovered that we were included in an open plan office with no privacy. I approached the Senior Local Director on the matter and he expressed the view that we should have no objection to such an arrangement. I asked him if he would like to work in an open-plan office, to which he responded, "Certainly not". The plans were changed.

In 1969 a customer from our Avenue Southampton branch came up with the idea of an annual boat show in Southampton, and the inaugural show began whilst I was at LHO. I was invited to join the branch Manager on a gin palace at the end of a small gangway with boats moored either side. We both enjoyed a few drinks until someone announced there was a force seven gale blowing outside. All the boats had slipped their moorings to avoid being battered against the pier.

Eventually, the time came for us to depart and we made a very unsteady way back along the gangway, feeling very exposed, to reach dry land, only to be hit by a huge wave which soaked us to the skin. So began the first Southampton boat show, which has now grown to a multimillion-pound international exhibition.

In February 1971 the country decided to decimalise the pound and I was required to assist in spreading the word on how the change would take effect. In my second role as general dogsbody, I found myself attending Mothers Union meetings to explain the changes. These meetings were often accompanied by some form of competition, which I was asked to judge: on one occasion I was asked to judge the most valuable coin and at another the oldest coin. I was far from an expert but it was interesting to see the ancient coins that were dug out by the members. My judgement was never questioned.

I think that I became the "expert" on decimalisation, and on one occasion was sent to Jersey to explain how the changes would take place. The Channel Island Managers were invited to a working lunch, which in accordance with Island standards was accompanied by wine and a port decanter that circulated after we had eaten. I spoke and dealt with questions as the port decanter continued to circulate, while some kind person kept my glass topped up. I have to say that I was not used to such hospitality and was delivered back to the airport in a semi inebriated state.

I had a good relationship with the other Assistant District Manager, and we had to cover for each other during holidays. I found his office a haven for unwinding as I could let off steam. He, however, visibly relaxed with a cigarette and never to my knowledge demonstrated the volatility that I felt. Perhaps there were some benefits to be derived from tobacco. On the other hand, I believe that the lending role was the more pressurised job. It gave me considerable satisfaction when I discovered that I was replaced by two A.D.M's advances when I finally departed to my next job.

From time to time there were gatherings of one sort or another attended by branch Managers and at one, to say goodbye to a Local Director, a man with a sense of fun and a former World War Two bomber pilot, we met together. With a few colleagues in a circle, glass in hand, I proposed a toast wishing the director well. I said I hope you will be very happy where you are going to, to which he responded, "And I hope you will be very happy where you are going". I had no idea that I was on the move and neither did my colleagues. Speculation was rife but I did not learn for some days that I was headed for the Channel Island of Jersey.

Eventually, I was called in to see the Directors and informed of my promotion to the role of Deputy Manager at the main branch in Jersey.

The current Manager was retiring and a new Manager had been appointed. I would be joining him in six months' time, but would have an opportunity to meet him for lunch before he took up the post. I would also need to visit Jersey to choose one of the vacant houses pending my move.

I duly visited Jersey to meet the departing Deputy Manager at his home. He lived in a lovely four-bedroom home overlooking St Helier, and knew all the houses on offer. Having seen the Deputy Manager's house, it was way better than the accommodation I had been offered, but it was not on my list!

I returned to LHO and informed the Senior Local Director that I had decided on the house I wanted but it was not on the list. I told him that I had looked at the Deputy Manager's house and that was my choice. He rose from his chair and said there were no circumstances in which I would be allowed to live in that house. I informed him that although I was a bachelor, I saw no reason why I should not be allowed to live in that property as I was fulfilling the same role as the present incumbent. We agreed to differ and it was left in the air. As the months went by nothing was said, but eventually the District Manager advised me that I could have the house, but the Local Director was not prepared to tell me! I think it would have offended his ego!

I should perhaps, at this stage, mention that having worked closely with the Local Directors I, unlike other Managers, had no fear of speaking frankly with them. There were, perhaps, occasions when I did not treat them with the respect that they thought they deserved. There were times when I could not conceal my disagreement, but I hope that I was never rude. The system of Local Directors worked well but in my view they should never put themselves on a pedestal to the extent that some were, on occasions, rather remote from the Managers with whom they came into contact.

A few of them had big egos and there were times when politics interfered with the efficient and smooth running of the business. Criticism was unacceptable, as I learned from a visiting Inspector who confided in me that he ended his career prospects when he reported on a Manager that, and I quote, "This report is not a criticism of the man, rather it is a criticism of those who appointed him". Suicide!

As the date for my move to Jersey approached, I sold my flat for £8,000, and placed the contents in store, as I would have to stay in a hotel for a period of time until my predecessor moved.

Looking back on my nearly four years at LHO, it had been a time of continued rapid growth in the volume of business. New branches, computerisation, decimalisation and the growing lending book, plus a move to new premises, ensured that I was never left with time on my hands. It was probably the most pressurised period of my banking career but none the less, very satisfying and enjoyable.

I had perhaps earned a reputation, particularly with my seniors, that I would not be bullied and would always speak my mind, even at the risk of blotting my copybook.

Chapter Twelve

Jersey branch

Year 1972
Prime Minister, Edward Heath
Inflation Rate: 3.27%
All Share Index: 193.39
Base Rate: 5%

My new job started with a bit of a shock. I spent a week with my predecessor who informed me, on day one, that he thought I ought to know that the Manager, my new boss, was having an affair with a member of the staff. I responded that I could not countenance such behaviour, but quickly formed the opinion that a) I had no proof and b) if it did not affect the banks business I should, perhaps, cast a blind eye over the matter.

My role as Deputy Manager meant that in addition to dealing with customers on a day to day basis, I oversaw staffing and the welfare of the staff. There were many staff over from the mainland, living in bank-owned accommodation, often sharing digs owned by the bank. As part of this role, there was a need to lecture those staff on moral standards, from time to time, and such lectures were not helped by the knowledge that the

Manager was himself misbehaving. That was a burden that I had to live with.

One of my early responsibilities was to represent the bank in the Royal Court, when we took security in the form of property. I was required to confirm to the Court that I knew the contents of the deed and had to nod my head as the deed was registered. The bank had a firm of advocates who dealt with the legal aspects of such matters and they informed me when I needed to appear. I think it was during my second appearance in the Court that I nodded my head and as I made my way to the exit, there was a loud stage whisper from the bank's advocate, "There's another one!" I returned to my place as the Jurat (Judge) announced the second "Do you know the contents of the deed?" Much to my embarrassment, I nodded my head, although I felt that all present were aware that I did not know the contents and was perjuring myself.

I was so furious that I had been placed in such a position that I insisted from then on that all deeds would be discussed before I appeared in Court again. I had just been observing existing practices, which clearly had become slapdash and which had placed me in a very embarrassing situation.

Working in Jersey, a tax haven, meant that we had a steady flow of wealthy immigrants seeking the benefits of shelter from a very punitive tax regime in England. I found the banking business very exciting as you never knew who you might meet. The experiences I relate are just a few recollections of business opportunities

I enjoyed. In 1972 there was a marginal income tax rate of 90% in the U.K., compared with a maximum tax rate of 20% in Jersey. Was it any wonder that the wealthy were attracted to the island?

One of the things it was necessary to come to terms with was the demon drink. On a busy day you might have lunch with a customer, attend an after-work drinks party followed by a round table meeting, which consisted of a meal at a regular hostelry with the accompanying alcohol. I took to sticking to Campari and soda, a rather bitter-tasting drink and very much an acquired taste. The drink had a fairly low alcohol content and you could constantly top it up with soda. I also had a policy, shared with the Manager, to leave any function before midnight. There was a steady stream of visitors to the island which gave rise to frequent lunches, both business and social. I often felt that my letters were couched in more powerful language if dictated in the afternoon.

There was one occasion when I broke my rule of leaving a function before midnight. A wealthy customer and his wife who had been involved in a dispute with the bank over investment advice, invited me to join them in celebrating the Chinese New Year at the best Chinese restaurant on the island. They provided the transport and I was reliant on them as to when we ended the evening. Despite hints from me, attempting to bring the celebration to an end, I did not arrive home until nearly four in the morning. I had to be up at six to catch a plane to Heathrow for a flight to Frankfurt. A substantial public company wanted me to attend a conference which involved a considerable bank funding facility, and with LHO approval I embarked on the journey. My plane out of Heathrow was delayed and I arrived rather late. The meeting ended about twenty minutes after I turned up and I returned to Jersey, via Heathrow, feeling very weary and questioning whether my journey had really been necessary.

Although we preferred to arrange all interviews with customers by appointment, there were occasions when someone visited unannounced. The unannounced were, more than often, the most interesting. On one occasion I was informed that a Mr Pontin was in the banking hall. I enquired if it was the Fred Pontin whose company owned a holiday camp on the island. It was indeed, he was not a customer and I cannot recall the reason for his visit, but we had a policy of always being available.

I subsequently met Sir Billy Butlin, who was a valued customer of the bank and who valued his relationship with Barclays, who had helped him over many years as he built up a multi-million-pound business. Sir Billy told me how he had remained a loyal customer of the Bank, which had become pivotal in the development of his business. I, in turn, told him that my first share purchase was in his company, which had provided me with a very good return. He had by then retired to the island and was well into his seventies.

One event that eventually gave rise to a rift with LHO, occurred when a gentleman called without an appointment. He was a multi-millionaire and a customer of National Westminster Bank. He had visited his own bank but had been turned away as there was no one available to see him. It turned out that he was investigating a move to Jersey and was seeking to borrow a substantial sum back to back, i.e. borrowing in England and depositing funds in Jersey as security. As a Jersey resident he would benefit from earning interest subject to a maximum tax rate of 20%, and could use the interest cost in the U.K, to offset his U.K. tax liability.

Here was, in my view, an ideal chance to gain a valuable new customer and I sought to obtain agreement from LHO over the phone. I was informed that I needed to prepare a formal application. The request was put together to go in the early post so that it would reach LHO the following morning. I took the precaution to mark the request URGENT so that I could tell the customer we had approval as soon as possible. Much to my annoyance, I received a call from a Local Director, without so much as a good morning, asking why I had marked the application urgent. Off the top of my head, I pointed out that it was new business and that it would save the customer about £50 per day. The phone was replaced and very shortly afterwards I was informed that my request had been approved. That customer was one of the best new business opportunities of my time in Jersey and came to us despite the delays imposed by Southampton LHO. There were times when I felt that some Local Directors were more concerned with their own importance rather than the growth in the banks business.

This very unsatisfactory experience was to return to haunt me at a future date when I attended a working supper to welcome a new Regional General Manager who was appointed to fill a new management role in London between the Local Directors and the main bank board.

There was a discussion with the RGM on the matter of the delay in getting advances sanctioned partly due to the postal delays. My Manager related a hypothetical example of the problem to which the RGM responded that it could be dealt with over the phone. That hypothetical example was, in fact, identical to my experience with the National Westminster customer. My Manager turned to me and asked me to relate my experience. I responded to the effect that I did not think we should deal with specific cases, which elicited the response from the Local Director, who was sitting next to me, "No, no, come on let's have all the detail". He was, in fact, the man who dealt with the matter and, having had a few drinks, I let him have it with both barrels. I recall saying that I did not get so much as a good morning having stopped everything to get the application in the post. There was an embarrassing silence when I finished and as the gathering broke up my Manager expressed the view that we might have upset the Local Director. In my own opinion, he asked for it, but we spoke to the Regional General Manager and expressed our concern. His response, "He will get over it". I think the RGM shared our view of that particular Local Director. The Manager having brought the Local Director to the event was not afforded the privilege of returning him to his hotel.

I believe, subsequently, that the Local Director attempted to teach me a lesson as he wrote to me concerning something else that was discussed at the meeting and on which he felt I had spoken out of turn. I responded that if he was unhappy with what I had said he should have said so at the time. There the correspondence ended.

I cannot say that following that meeting there was any improvement in speeding up the process, but we had made our point.

There were, over the years in Jersey, many occasions where doubts existed as to the integrity of some customers. We received an account transferred to us from the mainland of someone who I believe was of Greek nationality, and was informed that he was going to set up a "millionaires club". The concept was something that appealed to many, as there were many wealthy residents who had moved to the island and were looking for ways to occupy their time with like-minded incomers. Eventually, the millionaires club opened with pictures of the great and the good on the front page of the *Jersey Evening Post*, with appropriate headlines. My customer had confided to me that he intended to develop the club as a casino. I told him that there was no chance of operating a casino on the island as the only gambling that was authorised was something called "Crown and Anchor", that was played at the various fetes that took place on the island, during the summer months.

A week or so after the opening, the headline in the *Jersey Evening Post* read "Millionaires club closed. Gambling on the premises". It subsequently turned out that the premises, fitting out, food and drink consumed at the opening had not been paid for. A creditors meeting was called and it became clear that so many had wanted a share of the action that they had jumped in with both feet and little, if anything, had been paid to any suppliers. In those days, if anyone wanted to send someone to prison for a debt, they had to pay the costs. What my customer did not bargain for was that he would be shipped out of the island into the hands of the U.K. police, where he was wanted for other misdemeanours.

On another occasion, an existing long-established business was acquired by a rogue who was, I believe, endeavouring to asset strip, as the business had got into very serious financial trouble. The only way out seemed to be to sell the business on and I became involved with the disposal. The key aim was to get rid of the current management, as we were on the point of pulling the plug. It would have been a tragedy if the long-established company had not survived, and a buyer was found. I agreed that the bank would support a sale and agreed to a deal, which had the approval of the board, who were not really in a position to resist. The purchaser was a wealthy son of a valued customer and the sale was agreed on the condition that the bank was legally able to dispose of the company. Subsequently, a wealthy Canadian appeared on the scene with a better offer and the bank was threatened with an injunction if we proceeded with the original deal. I informed the original purchaser that the deal was off and LHO received a threat of the bank being sued for £250,000 if the original deal did not proceed. I had taken the view that the bank was not in a position to complete with the original purchaser as an injunction would have prevented it. To cut a long story short the deal was concluded with the Canadian and the business is, I believe, still thriving today. There was one condition of sale, and that was that the original rogue would have no involvement in the company whatsoever. Fortunately, the threat to sue was withdrawn as the father, a good friend of Barclays, told his son not to be so silly.

We always had to be on the lookout for crooks and fraudsters, and scrupulously ensured that new accounts were introduced by a reputable source. On one occasion I received a request to open an account which I agreed to do pending a letter of introduction. An account number was allocated but the issue of a cheque book was withheld. Subsequently, £25,000 was transferred into the account. Despite regular requests for a cheque book, the essential introduction was not forthcoming. Eventually, the customer appeared with a NatWest cheque book. I took the details and phoned the NatWest branch. The manager advised me that the customer had been introduced by the local firm of solicitors and it turned out that he was a new client who had come in off the street. I informed NatWest that I thought we were being subjected to a scam and we returned the £25,000 to the source from which it came. Nothing more was heard from the customer.

The branch was involved with a new company, set up with the help of the bank's trust company in London, to acquire a new roll on roll off ferry boat to operate out of Jersey to St. Malo. Shares in the company were offered to the general public and we, as a branch, were involved with the issue. The branch earned a good commission from our involvement, and in due course the new ferry boat went on its inaugural trip to St. Malo. I, together with the Manager and some members of our trust company, went on the crossing, and if ever there was a disaster in the making that was it.

The plan was that a number of vintage cars would drive onto the ferry but, unfortunately, the first car, owned by one of the Directors, drove up the ramp only to find the angle where the ramp joined the ship was such that the low slung Vintage Rolls Royce became suspended on the ramp unable to move forward or backwards. This caused a very long delay in leaving Jersey as the Director was anxious to avoid any damage to his vintage vehicle. On top of this no tickets, if there had been any, were checked and a tremendous number of gate crashers got on board. As a consequence of the delay and the gate crashers, the food and drink ran out and chaos seemed to reign. I am by no means certain that the ferry was not breaking any rules concerning capacity and the safety of passengers. The vessel eventually departed well behind schedule and on arrival in France, it was clear that the welcoming party, including a band, had gone home. As if things were not bad enough, the docking of the boat took a very long time as the French had picked probably the most difficult docking point for this new ferry. It is said, although I have no firm evidence, that a Senior Director of the company sacked the captain midway on the crossing, as he would not take a route that might have recovered some of the lost time. I believe that Maritime law ensures that the captain is in charge for all the time that a vessel is at sea. I think it became clear to all the bankers present that the company was unlikely to survive such a terrible start.

Whilst we always sought to do our best for our customers, some customers would often bring the occasional Christmas gift of a bottle of wine or something similar. We always acknowledged such gifts, but on one occasion I had dealt with a complex lending request which provided my customer with an opportunity to undertake a very profitable development. The facility was approved by LHO and one day my customer called in and dropped an envelope on my desk with a request that I share it with the Manager. He was gone before I was able to remonstrate with him. The Manager was out and I decided to open the envelope in front of a member of staff. The contents comprised £1,000 in £20 notes. I felt the need to place what had happened on record and I phoned LHO. Much to my shock, I was treated as if I had stolen the cash and was greatly offended by the LHO reaction. The Manager contacted the customer and suggested that a bottle of wine might be more appropriate. The cash was returned but subsequently two gold watches were delivered. I sat in on the conversation between the Manager and LHO. The Manager explained that the customer had presented us with two "small" watches and we did not wish to offend him by rejecting them again. Fortunately, the Local Director did not seek any detail about the watches but it is my belief that they cost more than the original £1,000. We were allowed to keep them.

It was during my Jersey posting that I met and married my wife. I also transferred to the Jersey Round Table and, seeking to get involved in the island, I volunteered for a position on the Round Table Council. I was given the task of Chairman of the Fetes and Charity Ball committee. I think the task was allocated to me as a new member and as I was totally unaware of what it involved! The fete that I had to run was a major event on the island in the parish of Gorey. It involved the personality chosen to adopt the island for the year, Bert Weedon, a popular guitarist of the time. I even had to give up banking for a few days to ensure its success. I recall writing a poem at the time for inclusion in a Round Table newsletter. I cannot recall all the details but the final stanza went as follows:

And now the Gorey fete draws near

And I am wishing I'd stuck to beer

At that fateful meeting months ago

Stand for council, no, no, no!

That just about sums up what I had got myself into.

Having achieved a reasonable degree of success with the fete, I had to commence preparation for the charity ball. This was again a major event on the island at which members of the Round Table put on entertainment after a dinner, and was a major fundraiser for our charities. I, who would never be seen dead on the stage, felt that I should set an example to my fellow tablers and volunteered to tread the boards. We were trained by a very camp musical director and had to take part in various dance routines. The rehearsals were joyous affairs, where we took the mickey out of the musical director, but we had to take the matter seriously, to ensure that it would work well and provide a good level of entertainment for the punters who paid for the expensive tickets. I can remember that we dressed up as lady dancers with male partners made out of stuffed models in dinner jackets, which were strapped to our feet. We performed a coordinated dance routine that went down well, although it was not up to professional standards. I seem to remember that one of the dances was to "Do you wanna be in my gang" sung by the now notorious Garry Glitter. The musical director was a lovely man and he dealt with the choreography and put up with a lot of leg-pulling from the many volunteers, all of whom were complete novices. The entertainment was a great success.

I chose a cruising theme for the event, having recently returned from a cruise with P & O. That company was very helpful in developing the theme and provided blank menu cards that we were able to use at the event. I also approached the local naval youth organisation and borrowed some antique marine equipment, including a free-standing ship's compass on the understanding that I would accept full responsibility for the valuable equipment's safety. Much to my horror, a member of the Hotel de France staff threw the ship's compass onto his shoulder not realising that the compass was not directly connected to its base. The compass smashed on the ground, glass and liquid in all directions. By great good fortune, I discovered that the manufacturers were still in existence and the hotel accepted full responsibility for its repair. In fact, the compass was returned in better condition than before, as there was an air bubble in the floating compass before the repair. To add to the theme, we decked out the steps leading to the hotel as a ship's gangway and had the sound of seagulls welcome the guests as they climbed the steps. I had never dealt with a themed evening before but was very satisfied with the outcome.

Every year the island organises the "Battle of Flowers", and businesses are invited to enter the competition. We decided that we should attempt to provide an entry in the form of a Barclaycard. A suitable, aged, lorry was hired and we purchased the necessary equipment to form the card, plus a supply of suitable coloured flowers to decorate the card on both sides of the back of the lorry. The main component consisted of marigolds, plus other suitable flowers of an appropriate colour. Unfortunately, the marigolds had suffered from some disease which meant that the top of the stalk rotted and the flowers were prone to break away if shaken. On the day of the Battle of Flowers, we received an urgent call for help as the lorry driver had changed gear badly and the lorry had shuddered removing many of the marigolds. We immediately sent reinforcements to use reserve flowers, and were indeed fortunate to receive second place in the commercial entries.

On one occasion, with the Manager on holiday, I received a call from our Uttoxeter branch, asking me to meet their customer the following day and show him around the island. I pointed out that we had a branch to run and did not do that sort of thing. When they explained the value of their customer I decided that we could make an exception.

The customer was Joe Bamford of JCB fame, and I made it to the airport in good time. I met Mr Bamford, who invited me to meet his co-directors in the new Hawker Siddeley HS 125 executive jet, which by that time was taxiing for take-off. With a waive from the Chairman, the plane came to a halt and I was invited into the aircraft for a very brief meeting. I understood that the plane was on its first flight following painting in the company logo and colours. Mr Bamford was like a kid with a new toy, and who could blame him. As we left the airport, he asked me if I would mind stopping the car as he had not seen it take off before. My day was spent touring the island with a charming man, lunch, and then delivery back to the airport. One of the highlights of my career.

My future wife worked for the bank, although not at the same branch, and we came into contact through the need to recruit as many new staff members from the Jersey schools as possible. I did not realise that I knew her father well, as he was my key source of recruits in his capacity as careers master at one of the major island schools. I can remember well the first time I joined the family for supper. They were all fast eaters and I am not sure whether I was subject to the third degree or that I just talked too much, but they had emptied their plates when I had barely started. My wedding took place on the 3rd August 1974 in a marquee, attended by many Table friends, staff, customers and family. Little did I know that the seeds of a future problem were sown on that day. My wife and I gave up the bank house and bought a brand-new property just outside St Helier for £32,000.

My relationship with my boss was a fairly cordial one, although there were occasions when things were not going well and he would nag at me as if I was directly responsible. We would reach a stage when I would get him off my back with a brief explosion of temper, but generally I had no complaints. He was a man from whom I learned a lot as he had the ability to do a deal with a customer and have him out of the door almost before the customer realised what had happened. He was a good frontman, although it was very clear he had a lot of time for the ladies.

The Chief Clerk mentioned one day that an attractive young lady who had recently lost her father was a regular attendee at the branch. He informed me that whenever she appeared the spy hole in the Manager's door was blocked. We examined the inside of the door and there was no hook or other device that might block the view. In fact, I told the Chief Clerk I did not believe him until the next time the young lady appeared when I checked for myself.

Quite exceptionally the Manager had been allowed to buy a Triumph Stag as a company car, something that did not accord with the rules of the scheme. The staff regarded it as a "passion waggon", and I think they knew more than I did of the managers outside activities.

Inevitably the Manager went too far, during his absence on holiday, one of my regular and valued customers called to inform me that he was removing all his business from the bank as a result of a member of staff having an affair with his wife. I told him that I knew who it was, and it turned out that my Manager met her for the first time at my wedding. There was nothing I could do to placate my customer but in my opinion the manager had breached the condition I had set whereby it would become necessary to report him. I immediately telephoned LHO to report the matter and was asked: "What do you expect us to do about it?" I responded that I did not know and was instructed to fly to LHO to discuss the matter. I related how I learned of an affair with a member of staff at the commencement of my duties and mentioned other related events. The Local Directors were asked to allow me to tell him the action I had taken rather than learn it from them. Fortuitously I was out of the office for the day when the Manager returned, and I broke the news informing him of my action and advising that I was out of the office for the rest of the day. I have never seen someone lose the benefit of his holiday so quickly as his face turned white and he told me that he was only a shoulder to cry on. I informed him that the Local Directors wanted to talk to him and left the office.

When I got home that evening I warned my wife that I might be on the move as I never thought we would be left together and I expected the Manager to keep his job, in view of his ability, and the need to avoid any sudden embarrassment, which might get into the local Jersey newspaper.

I understand that a decision was made at a very high level within the bank that no action would be taken, but I believe that the Manager's name came within a whisker of being used in divorce proceedings. The decision was also made that he and I should stay together, although

I went through a very difficult time as he ignored me completely for a long period. In the end, the bank's best interests were the main consideration of the action taken, and it is worth mentioning that the Manager was eventually promoted to Local Director!

I remained in my post to welcome the new Manager, but it was clear that my time was drawing to an end. At a meeting with one of the Local Directors, I was asked if I had ever had access to my report from the Manager. On hearing the Manager's comments about me, it became clear that he was trying to get his own back for my action in reporting him. I responded by pointing out that I had done the right thing for the bank and I was the only one to suffer. We had, in the good times, discussed the future and the Manager was well aware that I needed to move two rungs up the ladder to make up financially for the loss I would suffer in returning to the U.K. tax regime. The Manager was suggesting that I only deserved a one rung promotion and I made it clear that he would have won on all counts if such a job was offered to me. Although I did move up the two rungs, I was regularly reminded that I had held a pistol to the head of the Local Directors. I could not win!

The bank had recently introduced a business advisory service and I was sent on a nearly six-month course to learn all the techniques of advising businesses on how to improve their performance. The training programme took place at Selsdon Park Hotel, from which The Selsdon Group took its name. Selsdon Man was an expression used by Harold Wilson when he fought Ted Heath at the election, and the expression gained some notoriety at the time. As my first daughter had just been born I commuted to and from the island every weekend, building up a goodly supply of duty-free, which I stored in my car. We spent some weekends house hunting and eventually found a suitable property in West Wellow, near Romsey.

I found the training very useful and had the chance to put it into practice in Birmingham for a very brief time, before taking up the position of District Corporate Manager, which met my conditions for a return to the U.K. My role included undertaking business advisory reviews from time to time, plus playing a leading role as we sought to grow the Banks corporate business.

Much had happened during my five years in Jersey and I left the island with great regret. During my entire time in the Southampton region I had never stayed anywhere long enough to put down roots, until moving to the island. The bank business, despite the ups and downs, had always been exciting. I was now married and my first child had been born on the island. My wife and I had many good friends on the island and until the death of her parents, made many return visits. I had reached the age of forty, at which time you are required to retire from the Round Table. I had enjoyed the company of like-minded young men around my age and departed with many happy memories of my years as a Round Tabler.

Chapter Thirteen

Southampton Local Head office

Year 1977
Prime Minister, Jim Callahan
Inflation Rate: 5.22%
All Share Index.: 172.64
Base Rate: 14.25

As District Corporate Manager, I carried out Business Advisory Service activities, whilst encouraging Managers to grow the corporate business.

It was around this time that the bank had the chance to persuade the owners of the QE II that they should accept Barclaycard on their liner.

We met the appropriate staff members on board, and it was probably one of the easiest sales pitches I can remember. There were expensive items on display, including jewellery. I asked how many of these expensive items they sold, to which they responded, probably none! I pointed out that unless guests were carrying substantial cash resources, they could not make a purchase. With a credit card there was no limit to their ability to buy such items; there was little doubt that the point had been made and the card was accepted. I had never been on the QE II before and I have not been on it since.

Having moved back from Jersey with my wife, a daughter and a horse, I felt we had no alternative but to buy a property that could accommodate the horse. Following some search, we found a house with seven acres. A request was duly submitted to the bank for a loan to assist with the total cost of £56,000. Subsequently, I was invited to the Senior Local Director's room to discuss the loan. The Local Director informed me that head office were concerned as to whether I could afford the maintenance of such a large area of land. I pointed out that it was not all land and that there was a two-and-a-half-acre lake. "Is there?" he exclaimed: he was a keen fisherman. I said yes, and it is stocked with trout. "Really," he said. From then on there was no doubt that I would be able to afford the property. Once the property was acquired, I did a deal with the banks fishing club on the basis that they could fish with a maximum of three members at any one time on the understanding that they would restock it from time to time. It was the same Local Director who had informed me of my forthcoming move to Jersey at his leaving party. He had returned to Southampton in the senior position.

My wife and I learned to fly fish and I had a special fly, the name of which I cannot recall, which seemed to be very successful. There were occasions when I returned home to find fishermen who had not caught anything all day. I would put on my special fly and have two out for supper after a very brief attempt. I never disclosed the nature of my fly.

The property was purchased in October, and I soon found myself overwhelmed with grass in the spring. With only one horse I had to do something, and I followed the advice of a neighbour in purchasing six sheep. I also bought a book on keeping sheep, and so commenced a period of sheep husbandry, which I found to be the complete antidote to banking. We started with six ewes, bought a ram, and bred every year with the male offspring, which found their way to the abattoir, whilst the girls were retained for future breeding. I have never enjoyed roast lamb so much as eating the males that ended up in our deep freeze. When we eventually moved on, we had thirty-five ewes, plus the ram.

In those days, sheep were subject to dipping annually. I decided to build my own sheep dip and provided a dipping day when someone from the ministry of agriculture witnessed the dipping process. Without advertising the availability of the dip, I charged 50p per ewe, and sheep subsequently appeared from everywhere. I covered the cost of construction, plus chemicals used in the first year, and the numbers increased in future years as word spread.

The dipping day also afforded us the opportunity to compare notes with other amateur farmers and it became an enjoyable annual event. We also entertained the young farmers' group from time to time when they needed the space to enjoy some of their outdoor activities.

It was at an early stage of this activity that I attended a conference at LHO. During the proceedings, the door opened and the telephonist passed a note which moved around the table to me. I opened it up and read "Your wife phoned, she said, can you come home the sheep are out". I folded the note and continued with the meeting. By the time we had finished our discussions, I phoned my wife only to find she had rounded them up with the help of a neighbour.

My first daughter was born in Jersey and my second arrived some two years into my sheep management period. I had become accustomed to staying up all night during the lambing season and was ready for what the new addition to the family might bring.

It was around this time that a new Senior Local Director was appointed. Unfortunately, he and I did not always see eye to eye as he was very much a glass half empty man, whilst I was ever the optimist. I saw my role as one to encourage growth in our business on the basis that we were doing well, but we could do better. He, on the other hand, was dissatisfied with our performance and berated Managers on the lack of business growth. I continue to believe that mine was the better approach.

There was an occasion when a number of meetings were held in LHO, attended by a group of managers. The Senior Local Director addressed the first group on the need to visit businesses in their area, with there being no questions asked, apart from my intervention in which I stated that I believed that managers did not like "cold calling", an expression that he did not use. The point that I wanted to make was that with proper research a cold call could be made more fruitful, but I was never given the chance.

After the first group meeting I was called in by the Senior Local Director and informed that I had made no useful contribution to the meeting. I asked the Local Director if he thought it was a good meeting and pointed out that none of the managers asked any questions or participated in any discussion. I also informed him that many had said to me that I asked the very question concerning them. We left it at that.

The following day I attended the second meeting, where the Director changed his presentation, mentioning cold calling, and sought some response from those present. It was a much better meeting and he had the good grace to say as much after the managers had departed.

Sadly, my relationship with the Senior Local Director did not improve and I found that life became difficult under his regime. I was lucky to have the good life at home and knew that my days in my job were numbered.

One of the Local Directors called into my room one morning and asked me if I would call Regional Office and ask them if they really wanted me to put a particular memo in front of him. The contents contained included some basic errors and it had probably been written by a junior member of staff. I reacted strongly and informed him that I was being asked to do his dirty work. He responded that the memo contained mistakes, and I pointed out that we all make mistakes from time to time. He responded, "We don't pay Regional General Managers to make mistakes", and stalked off. I placed the memo at the bottom of my pile and sometime later the Director reappeared asking for the memo. He had clearly thought better of his action and told me he would deal with it.

Eventually, I was called up the corridor to be informed that I was being transferred as Manager of Cosham branch. The branch was an experiment that grouped three small offices under the control of one Manager. In the Senior Local Director's view, the system was not working and the group was losing money. The intention was to break up the group, and although the branch was currently the same grade as my existing job, the break up would ensure that it was downgraded.

I said that I did not want the job and enquired why I could not have the Portsmouth management job that was up for grabs. I was informed by words that I will never forget, "We have a young energetic man lined up for that job". I said that I would only go if Head Office said I must. There the matter ended, but I was called back in later to be informed that Head Office insisted that the move go ahead. I suspect that the matter was never discussed. I saw the writing on the wall and for the first time in my career contemplated resignation.

I can clearly remember my speech at the time of my departure. I pointed out that the last time I left LHO it was to a sunny island off the coast of France. Now I was going to a traffic island to the north of Portsmouth!

I left LHO with no regrets, but with a determination to get my career back on track. In my view, resignation was not an option, as I had very limited opportunities outside banking.

Barclays House – The Cake!

Barclays House by night

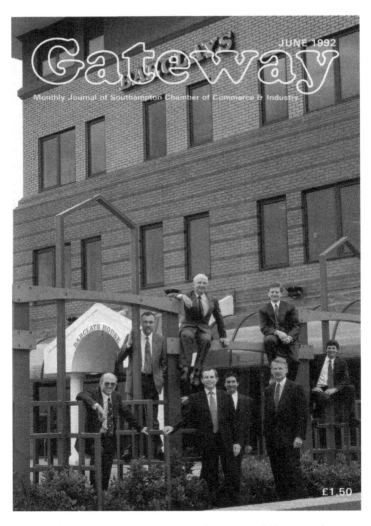

The Management Team on the cover of 'Gateway'

The New Branch Brochure – closed

VILLAGE OFFICE PARK at the following address

BARCLAYS HOUSE
P.O. BOX No. 2
OCEAN WAY
OCEAN VILLAGE
SOUTHAMPTON SO1 1TJ
Tel No. 0703 229911   Fax No. 0703 335792

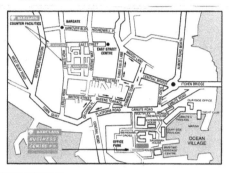

KEY FEATURES

- Experienced Managerial team and supporting staff able to respond swiftly to the needs of businesses be they sole traders or globally based companies.
- Small Business Unit and Business Banker service to cater for the special needs of the smaller business.
- Ease of access with ample free parking.
- Pleasant, efficient conditions in which to conduct business.
- Facilities to accept cheque deposits, computer data tapes and discs.
- Full range of financial and international services.

* Cash transactions will continue to be conducted over the counters at 30 and 171 High Street, Southampton.

The New Branch Brochure - open

Chapter Fourteen

Cosham branch

Year 1980
Prime Minister, Margaret Thatcher
Inflation Rate: 13.91
All Share Index: 283.82
Base Rate: 17%

Cosham was a challenge; the lending book was terrible and the number of cheques that were returned daily was at an all-time high. My predecessor was a high flyer who was destined for greater things. He had, however, not tackled the real problems, that were evident to me, after a very short time. Grouping of the branches was not really the problem, it was the accounting systems in place that were not working.

In order to break up the existing set up, the Senior Local Director employed a special researcher to provide a report supporting his proposal. In my view the report was flawed, so I prepared my own report which explained what was needed to make it work. The system operated on the basis of a record of all the transactions at the satellite branches being transferred to the main branch over a telephone link. Any brief interruption on the line meant that some of the records were not transferred. As a result, feeding the information into the computer resulted in a failure to balance. To resolve this issue the details had to be checked over the phone by calling back to the satellite branch. The system was terrible and needed to be altered. I ended my report expressing the view that under no circumstances should the existing structure be changed. Fortunately, the decision was made at Regional General Manager level, and we were given a year in which to turn the business around.

Rather childishly I was instructed not to tell the staff as a Local Director would call to break the news. I told the staff but asked them to act as if they did not know. We were off the hook for the time being.

The Local Director duly arrived and handled the situation badly. He made it clear that the branch was under the cosh and that we were essentially on probation. It was not the way I felt it should have been dealt with. It is worth recording that Cosham was an early experiment in grouping branches, and its eventual success possibly led to similar groupings taking place nationwide.

By this time the bank's computer systems had developed sufficiently to enable the satellite branches to feed their records directly into the computer, and the basic accounting problems had been overcome. We now had to start making some profits.

As I have mentioned previously, the branch, in an attempt to control a poor business, was returning cheques at an unacceptable level. I asked my Assistant Manager how much we charged for a returned cheque and what was the maximum we could charge. We were charging £1 and the staff handbook suggested the charge could be as much as £5. Income from that source alone increased by a factor of five, although it also resulted in a reduction in the number of cheques being returned as our customers counted the cost. This was no bad thing and it contributed to our efforts to clean up the business.

As far as I could see, the level of bank charges had never been realistic, especially when you take into account the time it takes to deal with many high-risk businesses, all of which was very time-consuming. The first time charges were calculated under my regime, there was a significant increase across the board. If such charges were unjustified, there would have been a backlash from customers, but there was little or no reaction.

In addition to increasing bank charges, there was a need to clean up the business and grow the lending book. A member of my staff informed me that he played squash with a company director who complained about his bank. I suggested that we should arrange a luncheon with the director, and we had a very fruitful meeting. The director was one of three brothers who ran a substantial house building company. They were following in their father and uncle's footsteps, but were seen by their bank as not warranting the fine lending margin enjoyed by the parent's company. It clearly irritated the young men and I offered to match the terms available to their parents. At the end of the luncheon the young director thanked us and said he would go back to his bank. Concerned that we might have wasted our time, I pointed out that we were offering them good terms and their bank should have been more forthcoming. The director said he would discuss the matter with his brothers who clearly were not happy with the way they had been treated. Fortunately, we won the business, which was to grow significantly and eventually take over the parents' business when they sought to retire.

There were other opportunities to grow the business, and steadily the branch was turned around. Once the year was up there was no mention of a breakup, but neither were there any congratulations on the significant achievement in that first year.

In year two the profits of the branch exceeded those of Portsmouth, and with the lending book much-improved, things were looking pretty rosy.

There was a customer who owned an electrical business in the high street. One day at an interview, I learned that he had a great interest in birds of the feathered variety. Somehow, we began discussing our domestic activities and I mentioned that I was contemplating introducing swans onto my lake. "I can get you two swans," he said. Within a matter of days he delivered two swans, wrapped in sacking sitting on the back seat of his Jaguar, which we released onto the lake. They had been pinioned so that they could not fly away. There was a worry that they might be attacked by the foxes, so I decided to dig a wide channel to form an island in the kidney-shaped lake. I returned home to find that the man with a digger had piled up the soil to the height of the house, but I had my island. In the end, we got in someone with a bulldozer to push the earth pile back into the lake at a suitable point that did not interfere with the overall shape of the lake. Despite the island, both swans were sadly killed by the foxes, although they were with us for at least a year.

I received a request to meet the Local Directors at LHO, my Assistant Manager said they are going to offer you the Portsmouth branch.

I suggested that they would not have the gall to offer me the job after what had been said at the time I was sent to Cosham.

As I drove to Southampton I thought about the possibility of being offered the Portsmouth branch, and decided how I would respond. The same Senior Director who had made the derogatory remark nearly two years ago, informed me that they would like me to go to Portsmouth. I was ready and responded by asking, "What's changed?" He responded, "What do you mean what's changed?" I pointed out that nearly two years ago he had informed me that a young energetic man was needed for Portsmouth and I wanted to know what's changed. His response was "Don't you want the job". Again, I responded to the effect that I was not sure and asked what the salary would be. As was usual at such interviews, he had no idea what my new salary would be. I also pointed out that much of the new business I had acquired would wish to come with me. He accepted the point and asked me to phone him with an estimate of the businesses likely to move. I informed the Directors that I would phone with the figure if they would at the same time inform me of my new salary. I had perhaps pushed my luck, but they knew I was deeply offended by the suggestion that I was old and past it at the age of forty-four.

I duly phoned the figures through the following morning, speaking to another director who had been present at the meeting. I think he was sympathetic to my feelings on the matter, but there was surprise at the level of business moving with me. I did, however, point out that Portsmouth was not very far from Cosham and most of the business that was moving had been acquired during my tenure. I was informed of my new salary, the level of which escapes me.

Chapter Fifteen

Portsmouth Branch

Year 1982
Prime Minister, Margaret Thatcher
Inflation Rate: 8.39%
All Share Index: 338.64
Base Rate: 14.38%

With my move to Portsmouth, I felt that my career was back on track, although there was the possibility that it might be my last promotion. Initially my office was in the main branch in Commercial Road, but following refurbishment of the Guildhall Walk office, I moved to the quieter part of Pompey, in which the management team was based.

I received a call from LHO asking me about a bomb. I enquired what bomb, only to be informed that the Guildhall Walk branch had been closed as an unexploded bomb had been located in a new development that was taking place in an adjacent property. No one on my staff had bothered to tell me that one of the branches for which I had responsibility had been closed. The problem was dealt with very quickly and the branch was out of action for less than a day.

Barclays sponsored the F.A. for many years and I was, from time to time, asked to present silver salvers to the player of the month, or the manager of the month. The first occasion was to Alan Ball whilst he was Manager at Portsmouth. I was invited, along with my family, to make the presentation and watch the match. My wife and daughters came down the tunnel to watch the proceedings, and we returned to the tunnel as the players prepared to start the game. What I had not bargained for was that all the practice balls were kicked into the tunnel, and we ended up dodging a cascade of footballs as we departed to find our seats. It was not until I had made the presentation that I realised how wound up some football managers get before a match. Alan Ball, was no exception. As someone who knows very little about football, I felt that the team should be more relaxed before a game, Portsmouth were, to my mind, wound up like springs, as was their manager, as they took to the field. I cannot recall who they were playing or the result.

The business at Portsmouth was very mixed, some good, some bad, with the bad being much more time-consuming. Steadily, and with the benefit of the business brought in from Cosham, the fortunes of the branch improved. My decision was to take a heavy hit by making early provision for bad debts rather than delay the process. If the debts were recovered then that could be regarded as a bonus, but once provision was made, the worst case was on record, hopefully growing branch profits would start to show through. There was also the consideration that I needed to identify accounts in trouble so that they would not count against my personal lending record. My attitude was always to assume the worst and face the future with better expectations.

After what I considered to be a good year, in which the underlying profits had improved considerably, I received a rather poor review because most of the profits had been written off by provisions for which I did not feel responsible. It seemed to me to be a very harsh decision, especially when I thought I was due a pat on the back. My view was that the early years were required to identify lendings at risk whilst increasing the underlying profit, which would continue to accumulate. Write-offs and provisions were one-offs and with them out of the way, the branch performance would leap forward.

I felt rather demotivated by the Director's comments. He was a man for whom I had the greatest respect, so I decided to write to him expressing my feelings about the review. My comments did not pull any punches, but I had thought carefully about the matter and did not feel that my reaction was unwarranted. I subsequently received a call from the Director and expressed the view that my memo was not written on the spur of the moment and that I meant every word of it. On reflection my response was perhaps rather rash, as he put the phone down on me. He was one of the few Directors I never wished to offend but I clearly overreacted to the situation.

Always on the lookout for new business, I secured an opportunity through a customer to meet the Chairman and board of a substantial PLC. I think the meeting took place at the Ritz hotel, but if not, it was another well-known London hotel. I arrived to find the group gathered in a circle near the bar. I was anxious to make a good impression and, after being introduced to the Chairman, I moved around the group introducing myself. There was a very young man in a smart suit who looked out of place, but only because of his youth. I shook him warmly by the hand and introduced myself enquiring as to his role within the company. He quickly informed me that he was the waiter and had come to collect the drinks order. If ever I wanted the ground to open up and swallow me, it was then. Needless to say, I gave up all hope of acquiring any business, but we had a convivial evening and I doubted, even in other circumstances, whether my efforts would have borne fruit.

There was a steady stream of business opportunities that came up and I recall putting two substantial cases to the local Directors. Both were declined, so I let it be known that I did not feel I was getting the support that I needed from LHO. A decision was made to agree to one of the submissions and inevitably the Directors chose the wrong one. I will not provide any detail as one company is doing very well today, while the other ended up in trouble. Sadly, I felt at the time that the Directors had made the wrong choice, but there was no loss that accrued to the bank, although the business that I really wanted is still going strong today.

My time at Portsmouth passed by very quickly but was not without the occasional brush with authority.

During the seven years I was at Portsmouth, I became President of the Institute of Bankers, which entailed running monthly meetings of the local group and organising the biennial dinner, which took place in the Portsmouth Guildhall. As I took over as President the committee was denuded of members due to staff movements and other departures. Fortunately, my staff stepped up to the plate and I remain very grateful for my staffs support at that time. A programme for the year was prepared and my main task was to find a good, amusing speaker to round off the speeches at the biennial dinner. I made endless approaches to well-known speakers including Geoffrey Archer, who I had heard before and who would, I know, have fulfilled the role to perfection. Whilst I was aware of some of his shortcomings, I was very impressed by a handwritten letter from him expressing his disappointment that he was otherwise engaged on that particular evening. It contrasted with the two-line typewritten letter from Jim Callahan's secretary declining my invitation. He was born and bred in Pompey.

As time was running out, I announced to my secretary that I would not be available to see anyone as I was determined to find a speaker by lunchtime. I worked the phone all morning and finally found a name that I did not know but who came highly recommended. After contacting a colleague, who undertook after-dinner speeches, I sought his assurance that the proposed speaker was good. He assured me that he rated him better than himself, so I decided to make the approach. I was fortunate to get a positive response and just had to hope that he would not let me down.

Fortunately, the arrangements for the dinner went without a hitch, I had to provide a copy of my speech to the Mayor's office, although there was no reciprocation. A General Manager from the Bank spoke and there were five speakers, including the Manager of the Trustee savings bank, who proposed a toast to the guests. In addition to staff and guests, the newly appointed Senior Local Director was also in attendance. My first and only meeting with the key speaker took place on the evening when he made the final speech. Any concerns that I might have had were very soon allayed as it was clear he had done his homework and provided a highly amusing speech which, in my limited experience, was one of the best speeches I have had the privilege to listen to.

The new Senior Local Director was full of praise for the event and I felt very satisfied with the outcome. A change at the top often brings with it a fresh attitude, and for the first time in my career I found a man who sought my opinion on matters. It was a very welcome change to be consulted and I enjoyed a very good relationship with the new Senior Local Director.

The bank had agreed to raise money for the U.K. Olympic team and it probably earned our Chairman his knighthood. Branch managers were asked to arrange fundraising events, and we decided to run a dinner aboard the HMS Warrior, Britain's first iron hulled armoured battleship, moored in Portsmouth docks. Whilst making enquiries we discovered our Chichester branch had got in before us. We decided to share the ship and did a joint venture, which was highly successful. As a result of our efforts, we were invited to a reception to meet Princess Anne. I had a committee to introduce to the Princess and could not recall all of their names as we had only met up infrequently. I warned them that they would have to accept whatever I called them, and the Princess moved rapidly through the gathered throng.

Having put down some roots in Jersey and with the children at a young age, we often returned to the island for our summer holidays. On one occasion, with the Olympics in prospect, we arrived at our favourite beach, Green Island, on the first day of our holiday. Our daughters were a little restless and I suggested a walk along the beach. To retain their interest, I suggested that we should see who could do the longest jump. A line was marked in the wet sand and they set about jumping. I pointed out that they needed to run up fast and leap into the air. Rather foolishly I offered a demonstration, which went wrong, and I landed on my right shoulder hitting the solid wet sand. There was a loud crack as I broke my collar bone and three ribs. As I writhed in agony, wet sand stuck to me everywhere. Fortunately, there was a nurse on the beach, who called an ambulance, and I was transported to St Helier hospital. The hospital staff seemed more concerned at the sand that I was leaving everywhere, but I was X-rayed and broken bones were confirmed. There was very little immediate treatment for my injuries other than a sling, and my ribs only hurt when I coughed or laughed.

I spent the rest of the holiday sleeping in an armchair and feeling very sorry for myself. Once I returned home, I had to have a driver for a short time and had to rely on sleeping tablets at night. After finding the need to adjust my rib cage when I woke, I consulted a doctor, who suggested doubling the sleeping tablets. This proved to be the answer, as I slept without moving position and the ribs started to heal. My long jump days were over, if they had ever existed.

As the years wore on, I decided that further promotion was doubtful and made the decision to move nearer to Portsmouth. We settled on a house on the edge of Hambledon which needed some refurbishment. There was a need to redesign the interior and we opted to build a swimming pool and double garage on the site to include a pool room.

At the time, an enclosed pool was free from VAT, and we purchased a plastic bubble which could be erected, or not, according to the weather. Although I did not like the bubble it kept leaves out of the pool in winter and allowed us to use the pool all year-round. It was perhaps a lucky break that the bubble was subsequently split from end to end, in the hurricane of October 1987, and we claimed on the insurance without replacement. It had saved us a considerable amount of VAT.

Before the arrival of the new Director I was asked to participate at a gathering of managers, which would be split in half and spread over two days. I was to give a talk on the preparation needed before a visit to customers. The then Senior Local Director opened the event and chose to mention a report on an account that was far too complex and should have been better presented. I recognised the report as one of mine and when my time came to speak I acknowledged responsibility, and reminded the Directors that we managers were sometimes under some considerable pressure to submit imperfect reports through time constraints. After the gathering, a Director whispered in my ear that my acknowledgement and subsequent comments were unwelcome. I responded that I would not repeat my response if the Director did not mention the matter at the next event. There was no climb down by the Director the next day and I repeated my response.

I think I was regarded by the Local Directors as a difficult man, but despite an unwillingness to toe the line, it had little impact on my overall career, and only resulted in a few brief setbacks.

Under my stewardship, the Portsmouth branch continued to perform well, and I felt no real desire for further promotion. I had a good quality of life and I had, perhaps, reached the pinnacle of my expectations.

It is just as you reach the comfort stage that something happens, and the new Senior Local Director saw in me something that others had not. I suppose management of the largest branch in the region should be the target of any ambitious Manager, but I was comfortable and settled at Portsmouth. I would not say that further promotion was unwelcome, but the thought of saying goodbye to my customers and starting afresh in another large city branch was challenging to say the least.

In due course I got the call from LHO and was informed that I was to be Business Centre Manager at Southampton City. Head office had insisted that the Directors interview two other Managers from other districts but I came out on top. It was a welcome boost to my ego.

Chapter Sixteen

Southampton City Business Centre

Year 1990
Prime Minister, Margaret Thatcher
Inflation Rate: 5.2%
All Share Index: 1225.80
Base Rate: 14.88%

I don't think that I have ever felt so mentally drained until after I said goodbye to my Portsmouth business, introducing my successor and then taking over the new Southampton business. I was taking over the branch from my old colleague, with whom I had worked in my early days at LHO. He was retiring from the bank and had been the Assistant District Manager (Staff) whilst I was Assistant District Manager (Advances) in the late 1960s.

Southampton Business Centre had some very large corporate businesses, which included Southampton Football Club. I had the privilege of two seats in the Director's box, which was set in the middle of the major stand at The Dell. If the supporters wanted to give the Directors stick they had ample opportunity to do so and, from time to time, there was banter from the supporters, which was mainly friendly in nature.

With the privileged seats came parking facilities, and I can think of no better way to watch football. At half time refreshments were provided and, from time to time, I would be invited into the inner sanctum, men only, whilst my wife or daughters stayed with the Director's wives. In those days football was very much a man's world.

At an early stage, it became evident to me that there was one account that was causing trouble to the staff. A company that maintained a substantial balance with the bank's treasury was involved with many currency transactions. The company would often make mistakes, blaming them on the bank, and we would have to stump up compensation. My predecessor had put up with it as the treasury funds helped to maintain one of the targets set for the branch, but I felt that the price was too high. I also discovered that the commission charged on the account had been cut to the bone, and all in all the business was not worth retaining with the customer dictating the terms. At the first meeting with the customer, having warned LHO that we might lose the business, I informed him that I wished to discuss the current banking arrangements. He immediately responded to the effect that he wanted to reduce the bank charges further. I made it clear that the bank could no longer operate on the existing terms and stated what the new agreement needed to be. We got off to a very bad start, and the business was soon moved to one of our competitors. The departure of the business did much for my credibility with the staff, as an unacceptable burden was suddenly lifted.

My career was not free from mistakes and I probably made my worst mistake whilst Business Centre Manager by taking over a lending from a competitor based on a balance sheet that was not what it seemed. Had I read the auditor's report, I would not have touched it, but the figures suggested a strong company, when clearly the auditors disagreed. Whilst I relied on the figures presented to me, I should have been made aware of the auditor's comments. I took the view that I was fully responsible for the lending, which was at risk, and LHO felt the need to put me on formal warning. I had no wish to blame any of the support staff and I was content to carry the can. This came as a great shock and hit my confidence badly. There was, in my view, a need to approach lending confidently, but having taken a hit I ensured that such a mistake was never repeated.

As the branch was the largest in the district, there was a view, which I shared, that the Business Centre should be located to more prestigious premises within the new Ocean Village development in Southampton. A brand-new office block with parking was located and agreed by the bank as the new offices. I set about changing the name of the block to Barclays House and the bank's premises department set about designing the interior to provide a management suite with dining facilities/ conference room, plus kitchen. Quite frankly I had never worked in offices that were quite so sumptuous. My room overlooked the Solent, and I had a privileged view of watching the QE II and other liners float into view. Once again, I had my own parking space and we had adequate parking for all visitors and staff.

I have mentioned only a few names in this book as I believe that I should only name those who I hold in high regard, and avoid naming any staff members. After some weeks I had the opportunity of meeting my customer Lord Montague, who owned the Beaulieu Estate and Motor Museum. I mentioned that my only interest in cars was that I had a Morgan car on order and had visited the factory. Lord Montague responded that he had just ordered a Morgan for his son and that Peter Morgan, the chairman, was coming to supper in a week or two's time. I was invited to take a friend to the supper and attend the talk given by Peter Morgan afterwards.

Lord Montague lived in a portion of Palace House on the Beaulieu Estate, but I was not familiar with the entrance. My colleague and I climbed over hedges and flower beds as we searched for the front door. We had entered by the public entrance to the motor museum rather than Lord Montague's private entrance. The supper was a most interesting affair as the Morgan Car company had very recently been visited by Sir John Harvey-Jones for his TV programme "Troubleshooter". I had seen the programme and agreed with Peter Morgan that the programme had not been a great success as far as the Morgan Car company was concerned. I learned, first hand, Peter Morgan's view of the programme and understood fully why he would not allow the programme to return to the company for a follow-up.

Part of the charm of buying a Morgan car was that you had to wait your turn, which could take as much as eight years, before a new car would come available. Sir John wanted the company to increase production, automate and fulfil the order book quicker. It was, in my view, sensible to carry on with a long waiting list, in the knowledge that the company was making around a million pounds a year and had a full order book well into the future. I think that the company increased production by one car a week, but a hand-built car is an essential part of a Morgan's attraction. After the supper, we walked down to the conference facility where members of the Beaulieu Car club had congregated. The supper and talk given by Peter Morgan was one of the highlights of my time in Southampton.

Occasionally I was invited to take key customers to lunch at LHO, and I invited the Directors of Vosper Thornycroft to such a lunch. I picked them up from the company premises and drove them to LHO. To my horror, as they got out of my car, I realised that my golden Labrador had somehow had access to the back seat and their smart blue serge suits were smothered in dog hair. We brushed them down before lunch, and fortunately they were very understanding.

The move to smart new premises took place about a year after my appointment and we arranged a formal opening ceremony. I persuaded a local catering training college to provide a cake in the shape of the new premises, and asked a customer who manufactured promotional devices out of card if he could help with the production of a suitable card to announce the move. I knew what I wanted as I had seen a folded card that, as you opened it, moved from the old into the new.

A mock-up of my design was prepared and we decided to proceed to print. In my view the outcome was one of the best communications I had ever seen, and it drew many favourable comments. On the front was a picture of the old branch, but as you opened it the old slid away to expose a picture of the new premises. It says much for the company and its relationship with the bank that we were never asked to pay for the final print run. It seems hard to say, but such relationships do not exist today. How can you ever have a relationship with a computer?

The formal opening of the new premises was accompanied by a harp player and speeches, plus the cutting of the cake. One of my tasks as Business Centre Manager was to get as much publicity as I could, and we benefitted from the move with comments in the local press and front-cover coverage in "Gateway", the chamber of commerce communication.

A further development of the banks business involved some of the branches around Southampton becoming satellite branches of the business centre, similar to the set up at Cosham some ten years earlier. I decided that it might be appropriate to design a branch tie to draw the branches together, and I proposed a competition amongst the staff, on the basis that all entries would be judged by the staff and the first choice would win a bottle of champagne. Much to my surprise the staff chose a design that I thought was pretty meaningless, and I felt I had to overrule the decision in favour of the second choice. I awarded a bottle of champagne to both the first and second entries but we ended up with a tie that clearly represented Southampton, and there were no complaints. It does just show that you cannot always rely on a group of people to make the right decision.

It was during my time at Southampton that I was made a Fellow of the Chartered Institute of Bankers, the final cherry on the cake.

Other than those described there were few events that warrant a mention. Although, another new Senior Local Director had been appointed and I very much regretted the departure of his predecessor. The branch performed well as we sought to meet all our targets but there were, in my view, problems looming on the horizon. I have mentioned before the old adage that "my word is my bond", and I had considered that my mantra throughout my career, and indeed throughout my life. I was becoming increasingly uncomfortable with changes that were happening within the bank. Suddenly, we were informed that we could only sell bank products and as I had always done the best for my customer, I was not comfortable with products that I knew were either inferior or not the cheapest on the market. The bank started to pay staff on the basis of sales results, which encouraged an attitude of a sale at any price, something of which I could not approve.

I had been involved on a committee to look at ways of rewarding staff based on performance. We had concluded that branches should receive a lump sum based on overall profit performance, with the manager rewarding staff on the basis of their contribution to the success of the branch. Such awards would have been overseen by the

LHO, but the main board was not happy with the committees' proposals and wanted to link rewards directly to sales of services. This, in due course, led to performance-related pay and meant that customers were bombarded by staff attempting to achieve sales targets that had been set by the bank. It also meant that the support staff who had no contact with customers were not necessarily rewarded appropriately.

I expressed my concern to the new Senior Local Director and informed him that I proposed writing to the bank Chairman. At his request I agreed to let him see the letter before it's dispatch, but on seeking an appointment I was informed that he could not see me for a fortnight. I had never before been met with such a response, so I decided to send the letter without further reference. Unfortunately, I did not retain a copy of the letter but it pointed out that throughout my career I had always done the best for my customers and there had been a bond of trust that had always existed. With the proposed changes in bank policy, that trust was being eroded, and I would find it difficult to implement those changes in such circumstances. Payment by results in a banking environment was, in my view, a mistake, and I think that it was a policy that came back to bite the banks, in view of the miss-selling that occurred.

The decision to send the letter landed like a lead balloon in LHO, but I did not feel I could allow delaying tactics to interfere. The outcome was probably what I might have expected. There was no written response but I was informed that if I did not like what the bank was doing I could retire. A decision had been made that I would not, in any event, remain in post at Southampton and I was given the option of another branch or retirement. I chose retirement as I had completed forty years in the bank and would receive a full pension, i.e. two-thirds of my final salary. Much to my surprise, I received an additional tax-free lump sum of £30,000 by way of compensation for my early departure and, as a pensioner, my pension was subject to a cost of living increase, whereas had I continued with the bank, my salary would have been frozen. I think you could safely say retirement was a no brainier.

Over my years with Barclays, I had accumulated a number of shares which I sold immediately after retirement. I believe that I received just over £7 per share. The disposal was not done in anticipation of a decline in the value, but it is sad to reflect that many of my former colleagues are facing a very substantial fall in the value of the shares they retained, as the shares are currently around £1. It is my view that it will be a long time, if ever, before the shares will recover to previous levels. That is a sad reflection on the mistakes of the past, when the banks were greedy for profit at any price. The people responsible for those decisions have long since retired on handsome pensions and have never been held responsible for their mistakes. Such is life!

I left the bank with my head held high and I believe that subsequent events have demonstrated the significant errors made by all the banks at that time in the pursuit of ever-increasing profit. I hesitate to claim that I was right, but the huge penalties that all banks have faced for mis-selling would not have occurred had they not pursued a reckless selling policy, in which all participated. My letter may have been considered by many as foolish, but it allowed me to retain my self-respect, and gave me the chance to remove myself from a career which had delivered both satisfaction and enjoyment, something which I believe is missing today.

The bank had a change of policy, to the extent that it no longer funded retirement parties. As a consequence, there were few, if any, such events. I decided that I would have a party, having had much contact with many members of staff across the district. I do not know to this day if it was a mistake or a final kindness, but I never received a bill for the event.

I look back over the forty years with pride and satisfaction. That period covered handwritten ledgers and statements, with the gradual development of mechanisation and then computerisation. There was also the introduction of decimalisation, plus the credit card innovation. I have had the privilege of working through a period of unprecedented change in the financial affairs of this country. We have seen the stock market grow at a very rapid rate, with inflation in and out of control and Bank Rate gyrate from a high of 17% to almost nothing at all, at the time of writing this story.

The good years of banking ended when I retired in 1993 and will never return. I had enjoyed a freedom that is not allowed to anyone today, as we become increasingly ruled by computers. There was a time when a deal was done by a shake of the hand but we have, in my view, forgotten those standards of probity and are hampered by the need for endless rules and regulations, to provide safeguards to a nation that seems to have lost its moral compass. At one time criminals made their ill-gotten gains by robbing a bank, but today they rob the bank customers by computer and internet fraud.

Whilst it can be claimed that much progress has been achieved over the forty years of my career and the subsequent years of retirement, I worry that it has been achieved at some cost, in terms of job satisfaction, honesty and integrity. The constant effort to create huge wealth in the short term is placing the longer-term chances of developing a sound economy at risk.

About the Author

The author is in his eighty-fifth year and was employed by Barclays Bank for forty years. He retired from the Bank at a relatively early age and has lived in Hampshire since moving down from Essex to Southampton in 1963. Sadly his wife has suffered from semantic dementia for the past twelve years and has been in a care home for the last eighteen months. Until the pandemic he enjoyed golf, gardening and watching his five grandsons playing competitive sports. Hopefully those pleasures will soon return.